PENGUIN BOOKS

# ENGLISH HUMOUR FOR BEGINNERS

*Praise for George Mikes:*

'In all the miseries which plague mankind, there is hardly anything better than such radiant humour as is given to you. Everyone must laugh with you – even those who are hit with your little arrows' Albert Einstein to George Mikes

'Bill Bryson is George Mikes' love-child' Jeremy Paxman

'Mikes is a master of the laconic yet slippery put-down: "The trouble with tea is that originally it was quite a good drink"' Henry Hitchings

*Praise for* How to be a Brit:

'An instant classic' Francis Wheen

'I love it and read it cover to cover. Also has good tips for talking about the weather, not that we need them' Rachel Johnson

'This is the vital textbook for Brits, would-be Brits, and anyone who wonders what being a Brit really means. Pass me my hot-water bottle, please' Dame Esther Rantzen

'Wise and witty' William Cook, *Spectator*

'Brilliantly comical' Pico Iyer, *The New York Times*

'Full of the very best advice that any would-be Brit should need (and for those of us who have forgotten exactly how it is to be ourselves) it's a jolly good read' *Telegraph*

'Very funny' *Economist*

# About the Author

George Mikes was born in 1912 in Siklós, Hungary. Having studied law and received his doctorate from Budapest University, he became a journalist and was sent to London as a correspondent to cover the Munich crisis. He came for a fortnight but stayed on and made England his home. During the Second World War he broadcast for the BBC Hungarian Service, where he remained until 1951. He continued working as a freelance critic, broadcaster and writer until his death in 1987.

*English Humour for Beginners* was first published in 1980, when Mikes had already established himself as a humorist as English as they come. His other books include *How to be an Alien*, *How to Unite Nations*, *How to be Inimitable*, *How to Scrape Skies*, *How to Tango*, *The Land of the Rising Yen*, *How to Run a Stately Home* (with the Duke of Bedford), *Switzerland for Beginners*, *How to be Decadent*, *How to be Poor*, *How to be a Guru* and *How to be God*. He also wrote a study of the Hungarian Revolution and *A Study of Infamy*, an analysis of the Hungarian secret political police system. On his seventieth birthday he published his autobiography, *How to be Seventy*.

# GEORGE MIKES

# English Humour for Beginners

*Illustrated by Walter Goetz*

PENGUIN BOOKS

PENGUIN BOOKS

UK | USA | Canada | Ireland | Australia
India | New Zealand |South Africa

Penguin Books is part of the Penguin Random House group of companies
whose addresses can be found at global.penguinrandomhouse.com.

First published by André Deutsch Limited 1980
Published by Unwin Paperbacks 1983
This edition first published in Penguin Books 2016
003

Grateful acknowledgement is made for permission to quote from 'The Rum
Tum Tugger' by T. S. Eliot, reproduced with permission of Faber & Faber; and
from the letter to Maurice Baring and 'Henry King' by Hilaire Belloc,
reproduced with permission of Peters Fraser & Dunlop

Set in 10/12 pt Baskerville 10 Pro
Typeset by Jouve (UK), Milton Keynes
Printed in Great Britain by Clays Ltd, St Ives plc

A CIP catalogue record for this book is available from the British Library

ISBN: 978–0–241–97854–2

www.greenpenguin.co.uk

Penguin Random House is committed to a
sustainable future for our business, our readers
and our planet. This book is made from Forest
Stewardship Council® certified paper.

# Contents

# Part One: Theory

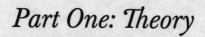

# Does it Exist?

ENGLISH HUMOUR resembles the Loch Ness Monster in that both are famous but there is a strong suspicion that neither of them exists. Here the similarity ends: the Loch Ness Monster seems to be a gentle beast and harms no one; English Humour is cruel.

English Humour also resembles witches. There are no witches; yet for centuries humanity acted as though they existed. Their cult, their persecution, their trials by the Inquisition and other agencies, went on and on. Their craft, their magic, their relationship with the Devil were mysteries of endless fascination. The fact that they do not exist failed to prevent people from writing countless books – indeed libraries – about them. It's the same with English Humour. It may not exist but this simple fact has failed to prevent thousands of writers from producing book upon book on the subject. And it will not deter me either.

We shall have to spend a little time on definitions. The trouble with definitions is that although they can be illuminating, witty, amusing, original and even revolutionary, there is one thing – and perhaps one thing only – which they cannot do: define a thing. This is more true in the case of humour than in the case of anything else. We shall come to that later. But we shall still have to try to answer such questions as: What is English? What is Humour? What is English Humour? Is English Humour the humour of a nation or just a class? What have cockney humour and Evelyn Waugh in common?

Before going into details, I should like to say a few words in general. If English Humour is the sum total of all humorous writing that has appeared in the English language then, in that sense, English Humour does exist. So do Bulgarian, Finnish and Vietnamese humours. England – or Britain, or the British Isles – has produced eminent and brilliant funny men from Chaucer, through Dickens, Oscar Wilde and W. S. Gilbert to P. G. Wodehouse and Evelyn Waugh. And, if the question is whether the English people can laugh and make good jokes, then again the answer is yes.

But this is not what champions of English Humour have in mind. They allege that the English possess a sense of humour which is specifically English, unintelligible to, and inimitable by, other people and – needless to add – superior to the humour of any other nation. That is a debatable point. But a point worth debating.

In other countries you may be a funny man or a serious man; you may love jokes or hate them; you may think clowns and jesters the cream of humanity or crushing bores. You may, of course, have the same views in Britain, too. Yet Britain is the only country in the world which is inordinately proud of its sense of humour. In Parliament, in deadly serious academic debates, even in funeral orations, Shakespeare is less often quoted than Gilbert or Lewis Carroll. Every after-dinner speech – be it on the sex-life of the amoeba – must end with a so-called funny story. You may meet here the most excruciating bores, the wettest of blankets, the dreariest sour-pusses all of whom will be extremely proud of their sense of humour, both as individuals and as Englishmen. So if you want to succeed – indeed, to survive – among the British you must be able to handle this curious and dangerous phenomenon, the English Sense of Humour; to stand up to it; to endure it with manly or womanly fortitude.

In other countries, if they find you inadequate or they hate you, they will call you stupid, ill-mannered, a horse-thief or a hyena. In England they will say that you have no sense of humour. This is the final condemnation, the total dismissal.

On the following pages I shall explain what English Humour is, i.e. what it is if it exists at all; what the English think it is; how to be humorous in England; what insults and insolence one must pocket lest one should be declared humourless, i.e. not a member of the human race.

# If it's Good it's English

MY FIRST SUSPICION that there is no such thing as English Humour arose early. A few weeks after my arrival in 1938 a few people told me that I had a very English sense of humour. That was obviously a compliment. Even more obviously it was utter nonsense. I had just arrived from Hungary where I had been bred and born; I had never read one single book in English because my English was not good enough; I had seen altogether three Englishmen in my life, none for longer than for five minutes. How, where and why should I have acquired an English sense of humour?

I observed, however, that only my good jokes were greeted with this high praise. No dud joke, witless observation or silly pun ever merited the comment. No one ever said: 'Your sense of humour is absolutely lousy but, I must say, it's very English.' The pattern about my humour followed the general pattern: if it was good it was English; if it was abominable it was foreign.

But soon enough contrary doubt assailed me, too. Perhaps, after all, there *was* a special English sense of humour. I heard the following joke in those early days.

Two men are standing on the platform of Aldgate East underground station – two cockneys, as they must be in any Aldgate East story – at 11.30 at night. There is only one other person there, a shabbily dressed individual at the other end of the platform.

'Ð'you know who that chap over there is?' asks one of the men.

'Who?'

''E's the Archbishop of Canterbury.'

'Don't be a fool.'

'I tell you 'e is. The Archbishop of Canterbury.'

'Look, Bert, what would the Archbishop of Canterbury be doing at 'alf past eleven at night, waiting for a train at Aldgate East? Dressed like that?'

'I 'ave no idea what 'e is doing. But I've often seen his pictures and it is 'im all right.'

'I bet you anything 'e ain't the Archbishop.'

'A quid?'

They bet a pound and Bert walked over to the other man and spoke to him.

''Scuse me, but do you 'appen to be the Archbishop of Canterbury?'

'Am I who?' the man asked darkly, and did not seem to be amused.

'The Archbishop of Canterbury.'

'You — off, but quick. Mind your own bloody business and go to — hell.'

Bert walks back to his friend and declares: 'The bet is off. You can't get a straight answer out of him.'

I thought this joke was quite amusing but, much more to the point, very English. Why? First, there is this lovely nonsensical element. Bert's friend had a good point there: what would the Archbishop of Canterbury be doing at an East End underground station, shabbily dressed, at half past eleven at night? The courtesy of the question, addressed to the third man, is very English, too. So is the betting. But what makes it a really English joke is its pseudo-fairness. If there is one accusation the English resent as much as not having a sense of humour, it is that they are not fair. Meet an English murderer in jail. He will readily admit that he has slain seven people in the pursuit of his trade. But accuse him seriously of being unfair in some concrete matter – of jumping a queue, for instance – and you will be the eighth victim. In connection with British justice – also claimed to be the best in the world – there is a saying: it is not enough that justice should be done, it must be seen to have been done. This really means never mind justice, the main thing is that your decision should *look* just. This joke reflects the same mentality. Bert – in the jokes of other countries – would have come back and said: 'The chap is a foul-mouthed lout, it cannot possibly be the Archbishop of Canterbury. You win.' That would have been right but stupid. To say: the bet is off etc is very English and very clever.

# What is 'English'?

AND NOW back to definitions. 'English' in this book means English, Welsh and Scottish but not Irish – so I should, perhaps, call this book *British Humour for Beginners*. But who on earth has ever heard of 'British' humour? I am sure even the fiercest Scottish nationalist will agree that English humour is English humour.

I know very little about a specific Welsh sense of humour but as probably more Welshmen – or people of Welsh origin – live in England than in Wales, I take it that they are, on the whole, sufficiently anglicized to be absorbed by English humour-imperialism.

About the Scots I am going to make a daring statement which may cost me my life. I know they are a separate nation; I know that many of them plan to become even more separate. I have, in fact, a soft spot for the Scots, have always got on splendidly with them and, like all Hungarians, find it easier to learn Scottish English with its harsh consonants than the softer English variety with its unclean vowels (even in the speech of the highly educated classes). If you observe the Scots from within the United Kingdom you can easily perceive the differences between them and the English. But observed from the Continent of Europe they resemble the English much more than they care to. Unless they wear a kilt – and who wears kilts nowadays except Sunday-Scots in Trafalgar Square during the tourist season, or visiting English manufacturers of plastic mugs in the Highlands, plus one Hungarian I know – well, unless they wear a kilt they are, in the eye of the foreign observer, totally indistinguishable from the English. What does a man from Frankfurt or Warsaw see when he looks at the English and the Scots? People who speak the same language; people with the same manners, the same shyness and reserve (at least when abroad), the same arrogance (at least when abroad), the same feeling of superiority. And the fact that the Scotsman feels superior to the Englishman as well as to the rest of the world while the Englishman tends to ignore the Scot means little to the man of Frankfurt.

Yes, I repeat – even if I am stabbed to death in the streets of Glasgow – that to foreign eyes the Scots are almost indistinguishable from the English.

Nevertheless, we have all heard about the taxi in Aberdeen which got involved in a regrettable accident and eighteen people were injured in it.

Or we have all heard jokes like this one:

The Scotsman (in the distant past) arrived in London with three pieces of luggage. He asked the porter at the station what his charges were.

'Fivepence for the first piece, threepence for the others.'

'Very well, I shall carry the first one, you the second and the third.'

In other words, what about the proverbial meanness of the Scots? Surely, writing a book on humour, one cannot ignore *the* Scottish joke?

I think one can. First of all, jokes of this kind are monotonous. Secondly, they are jokes *about* the Scots, not *by* the Scots, so they have little to do with the Scottish sense of humour. Thirdly, the Scots used to be poor and the (then) rich English mistook their poverty for meanness. According to my own experience the Scots are, in fact, particularly hospitable and generous.

I doubt (as I have already explained) that there is such

a thing as an English sense of humour, consequently the – say – Welsh sense of humour would be a sub-species of a non-existent genus. But that would be in the true English nonsense tradition. Until the nineteen seventies there was a coin in circulation in Britain called the half crown. There was no crown, but this disturbed no one. The English were quite happy with a fraction of a non-existent unit. In mathematics half of nothing is nothing. In humour and in British fiscal matters (the two are often identical) half of nothing is quite something.

# The Irish Joke

‖◄◗◄◗◄◗◗◗❖◗◗◗►◗►◗►◗‖

THERE ARE TWO CLOCKS on a tower in Dublin. An English visitor points out to an Irishman that the two show different times. The Irishman replies: 'What's the point in having two clocks if both show the same time?'

Or: An Irish traveller dies on a boat and has to be buried at sea. Later the Captain reports with regret that twenty sailors died digging his grave.

These are typical Irish jokes. Like most Irish jokes they try to make the point that the Irish are stupid – the other Irish jokes try to prove that they are lazy.

When I first came to England my English was quite sufficient to get along with in Budapest, so I thought it was good, but I found that London English differed quite considerably from Budapest English. But whatever mistaken ideas I may have had about my knowledge of the English language I was aware of knowing very little about the British people – not exactly an advantage for a working journalist. I and my Hungarian colleagues knew that the Scots lived up there, somewhere in the North; we knew – from a famous nineteenth century allegorical poem by János Arany – that the Welsh existed, although we were not sure which parts of the island they lived in; and we knew – we loved our Bernard Shaw in Hungary – that the Irish occupied John Bull's other island (or to put it more precisely, that John Bull occupied that other island which the Irish regarded as their own). That was more or less the sum total of our ethnological knowledge.

Our greatest and most urgent preoccupation was to learn English and to acquire some knowledge about the peoples of these islands. It was a sensational event when one of our colleagues decided to visit Ireland. When he came back we besieged him with questions. What were the Irish like? He was puzzled.

'They are an amazing lot. They are exactly like the Hungarians but they all speak fluent English.'

I have yet to hear a better description of the Irish. Now, forty years on, I still think that definition holds good. Consequently, the Irish are near my heart and I have always resented the sneering racist flavour of Irish jokes.

So what about these jokes? Are *they* all right or is my resentment right?

I think both are wrong.

The Irish probably *are* lazy but this fact points to their intelligence not to their stupidity. A small minority of people are lucky enough to make their living by doing things they like doing – but even they do not like everything they have to do and do not always like working. The majority simply have to sell their labour, their expert knowledge, their skill, their time or just their physical strength. That is a bargain and most of them keep the contracts they have made. But why on earth should people *like* dull jobs? And if they do, why should this be the sign of intelligence and not stupidity?

Besides, who are the English to laugh at the Irish, or at anyone else for that matter, because they are lazy? They are intelligent enough to be lazy themselves. And why should they laugh because the Irish are supposed to be stupid? I have mentioned Shaw, an Irishman who for seventy years called the English the stupidest race in the world and made a good living on it, most of his money contributed by the English themselves. Once upon a time, immediately after the war, the Germans used to work very hard but they had good reasons and a good purpose for it. The mood did not last long. They have come to their senses and today they are as lazy as the rest of us.

The Irish are not lazier and not stupider than most people. Some of the greatest writers in the English language – Swift, Wilde, Shaw, James Joyce, Yeats, just to mention the first five of the dozens of names that come to one's mind – were Irish. So surely we ought to cry 'racism!', 'unfair!', 'disgusting!' and swear never again to tell or even listen to an Irish joke?

Until a few years ago I should have approved this proposition. Then I was invited to a party in a large country house. The guests were dispersed in many rooms. In one of these rooms, with its door open, I found myself with a group of six or seven people and told them a joke about homosexuals. The laughter was silenced by a man who suddenly appeared from the corridor outside and roared with flashing eyes: 'Who told that homosexual joke?'

I said it was me.

'I am a homosexual!' he shouted. He sounded very proud of it as if it were a major achievement.

'So what?' said I.

He seemed to be stupefied, I think he was convinced that I had failed to hear what he had said, so he repeated it even more loudly: 'You've just told a joke against homosexuals and I am a homosexual.'

This was obviously a gimmick of his, he must have said it many times before.

'No,' I told him, 'I didn't tell a joke against homosexuals. But people constantly tell jokes about Jews, about the English, about the Germans, about the Irish, about the Scots, about prostitutes, about the new-rich, about doctors, about the Queen and – perhaps in more questionable taste – about stutterers. Why should homo-sexuals be the one and only exception? What is so specially sacrosanct about them?'

I failed to convince that man whose main contention seemed to be that he was no German, no new-rich, no Queen, no stutterer: he was a homosexual *ergo* it was wicked to tell jokes about homosexuals. But I think I was right. I do not say that all these jokes are innocent; some of them are truly vicious. But when they are told innocently, we must accept them simply as the expression of some stereotyped opinion the aim of which is to raise a laugh. Occasionally they may do harm and incul-cate hostility against one group or another. But, on the whole, while racists may be fond of racist jokes, jokes will not turn people racist. I think we ought to be toler-ant, and try not to be what the Germans call *tierisch ernst*, brutishly serious, not to be self-righteous and outraged when we hear a joke against a group we happen to like and then proceed to tell jokes against groups we happen to dislike. After all, while jokes should be taken seriously, they should not be taken *that* seriously.

And there is another aspect of this. In Australia I once heard a particularly loud-mouthed and ill-educated group of Aussies amuse themselves by telling a string of anti-Italian jokes. Slowly I grew as irritated as that homo-sexual chap had been at the party. The Italians I had met in Australia were decent, hard-working people, most of them much more intelligent than these particular Aus-tralians. Then it suddenly occurred to me that it was not hatred of the Italians that made them tell these jokes, but love of themselves. They wanted to feel superior and clever, and anti-Italian (in fact, anti-anybody) jokes achieve such a purpose. Poor bastards, I thought then, if you need these jokes as therapy to bolster up your ego, you must have them.

\*

A motorist has taken the wrong turning and is completely lost in the depths of County Cork, Eire. At last, he discovers a local man and asks him how to get to Limerick.

The man scratches his head and replies: 'Well, if I wanted to go to Limerick I wouldn't start from here.'

# What is Humour?

WHAT IS HUMOUR?

I do not know.

Mr Spike Milligan, the comedian, wrote: 'Comedy is a way of making money. The trouble is that everyone nowadays tries to make it into a philosophical system.' He was quite wrong. Humour is philosophy, the trouble is that everyone nowadays tries to make money out of it. This, however relevant, is beside the main point. The point is that great minds, from Aristotle through Bergson and Freud to Mr Milligan, make desperate, and often brilliant, efforts to define humour and they always fail.

The definition of humour is a problem of philosophy. Therein lies the first difficulty. Having heard the word 'humour' people expect a good laugh. This expectation is unjustified. The philosophical definition of humour should not be any funnier or more entertaining than the philosophical definition of the purpose of life.

But – and therein lies the second difficulty – efforts to give a definitive answer to the question, what is humour, are just as vain as efforts to give a definitive answer to the question, 'what is the purpose of life'. On this latter question thousands of tomes have been written by some of the best brains of humanity. The answers given were often brilliant, exciting, thought-provoking and profound, but never do they seem convincingly to be true. (Perhaps the truth is just too dull and uninspiring to hold the attention: life has no purpose? But one can't even swear to that.) The achievement of philosophy is asking the right questions and giving the wrong answers. The achievement of philosophy is to skate with breath-taking skill around problems and to find no solutions. We are no nearer to finding a convincing and generally accepted answer to the question 'what is the purpose of life' than we were half a dozen millennia ago. The same goes for the problem of humour.

I am not going to fill this gap here and now. I am not going to find the solution missed by so many, from Aris-totle to Milligan. Neither am I going to sum up the innumerable theories (except for touching on a few, when it is inevitable). I cannot completely ignore the subject of defining humour but it is not my main subject. My main subject is: how to try to be funny in England. So I am going to sum up and paraphrase what I have said in some earlier books* on the subject. My medita-tion will raise me into the august company of Aristotle, Bergson and Freud. They could not solve the problem; neither can I.

What is humour, then? Well, what is rain? It is something different for the meteorologist and the farmer. For the bank clerk it may be the phenomenon which makes his weekend miserable; for the cinema-owner it may be the phenomenon which makes *his* weekend profitable. And are a drizzle and a downpour, a shower, a cloud-burst and a drop here and there all rain? Is the difference between a drizzle and a deluge a difference in degree or does it amount to a difference in kind? One can maintain the difference is only one of degree – although one can

---

* *Eight Humorists*, with drawings by David Langdon, Wingate, 1954 and *Humour in Memoriam*, Routledge & Kegan Paul and André Deutsch, 1970.

hardly expect the wrongdoers of antiquity who perished in the Deluge to agree. One can also say that whatever different angles different individuals may have, rain is still rain, and scientific definition will lead to precise results.

But this is not true. There is nothing magic about science and in particular nothing magic about methods which claim to be scientific. Different sciences may reach different results even when dealing with the very same case. Legal insanity, for instance, is very different from medical insanity. Physicians may diagnose a man as sick; judges may treat him as a criminal. Medically he may be an invalid; legally he may go to prison for life or, in some countries, he will be hanged.

Similarly, one of the several difficulties about humour is that people approached it from several angles. Aristotle looked at it from an aesthetic point of view, Bergson as a philosopher and Freud as a psychologist. It is the story of rain, all over again.

You may know many things about humour; you may use it with deadly or uproarious effect; you may enjoy it or earn your bread with it; you may classify it into comedy, wit, joke, satire, irony, mimicry and so on almost indefinitely and you may discover penetrating truths about it. But you still do not know what it is. Similarly, physicists can produce electricity; they know all about it; with its help they can travel in the air, on land or on the water; they can dig tunnels, remove mountains, transmit messages over thousands of miles; they may reach the moon and build miraculous computers; they can lighten our darkness and cure the sick with it; but they do not know what electricity is.

Let us, then, try another approach and seek an answer by way of elimination: *what humour is not*?

The more famous treatises on the subject we read, the nearer we come to our aim. Indeed, the most reliable

FREUD
NICOLSON
BERGSON
Koestler
EASTMAN
Aristotle

general definition of humour would be: humour is not what the great minds of humanity have said it was.

Bergson's book on *Laughter* is excellent reading – much better than its summaries. It is full of diversions and the diversions are the best part of it: funny, witty, often brilliant. What he has to say on the main subject, however, is occasionally downright silly.

Bergson's main ideas are elasticity, adaptability and the *élan vital*. The opposite of these, inelasticity and rigidity, are laughable, indeed one definition of the laughable is 'something mechanical encrusted upon the living'. That means, as Arthur Koestler pointed out, that the funniest things in the world according to Bergson are the automaton, and the puppet on a string, the Jack-in-a-box, etc. Koestler said, in effect, that if Bergson was right, Egyptian statues, Byzantine mosaics, epileptic fits, even other people's heartbeats would turn our lives into perpetual merriment.

Bergson goes on to analyse all varieties of humour, and to find that there is an element of inelasticity in everything that is funny. This is an intellectual exercise and people of my generation, used to watching Marxist ideologists performing on the flying – or lying – trapeze, explaining that poverty is riches, compulsory silence is freedom of speech and oppression is liberty find nothing extraordinary in it. Many of us have learnt the trick. Give us an attractive-sounding, apparently clever idea and we will apply it to anything. It is an easy exercise and Bergson does it brilliantly. In the course of his reasoning we find statements such as: all clothes are intrinsically ridiculous. Happy is the man who looks at his socks in the morning and is cheered up for the rest of the day. He also finds physical deformity funny, if it can be successfully imitated. A hunchback resembles a man who holds himself badly, so he is funny. A black man is also funny because he looks as if he has covered his face with soot. Bergson asks us: why do we laugh at a head of hair which has changed from dark to blonde? But do we? Personally I don't. What, he demands, is comic about a rubicund nose? Nothing, if he asks me. Why do we laugh at a public speaker who sneezes at a crucial point of his speech? Where lies the comic element in a quotation from a funeral oration: 'He was virtuous and plump'? It lies, Bergson explains, in the fact that our attention is suddenly called from the soul to the body. Any incident, we are told, is comic, if it calls attention to a person's physical qualities, when it is the moral side that really concerns us.

This is utter balderdash and offensive balderdash into the bargain. Physical deformity is not funny under any circumstances, however easily it can be imitated. It is no good trying to fathom *why* a black man looks funny. He does not look funnier than a white man or a Chinese and I know several people who went to Amin's Uganda, which is full of black people, and failed to roar with laughter even once, from dawn to dusk.

He also says: an individual is comic who goes his own way without troubling himself to get into touch with his fellow beings. 'It is the part of laughter to reprove his absent-mindedness and wake him out of his dream.' There may be a great deal of truth in the suggestion that some of the great comic characters, like Don Quixote, were not adjusted to reality. But this is not to say that all of them are unadjusted, from the women in *Lysistrata* to Bertie Wooster. And why bring absent-mindedness into it? Surely, absent-mindedness is not an indispensable element of humour, except in those overworked professor jokes. Don Quixote may have been maladjusted; he was not absent-minded.

Bergson's worst failure begins with his doctrine that laughter is always corrective, intended to humiliate. So far so good; the aggressive, often cruel, nature of laughter is not in doubt. But the deduction he makes from this assumption is that as a result of this it is impossible to laugh at oneself. Whereas it is indeed not only possible, but – for the very survival of the human race – it is necessary. A sense of humour – and I shall return to this theme – begins with one's ability to laugh at oneself.

It might be said in Bergson's defence that his idea that deformity and Negroes are hilarious is out of date. But he was a twentieth century author – he died during World War II – and he has little excuse for being considerably more out of date than Aristotle.

Freud in his discussion of humour declares that an important element is *economy*: a thesis which I view with doubt. He gives us various jokes in his book: 'The girl reminds me of Dreyfus. The army doesn't believe in her innocence.' This may be the funniest way of calling a woman a whore but not, surely, the most economical? He tells us about two American businessmen of doubtful honesty who had their portraits painted. When a famous critic saw the two of them hanging side by side, all he said was: 'Where is the Saviour?' It was a witty way of calling the two gentlemen thieves, but was it an economical one?

Freud says that not all wit is aggressive and he distinguishes between harmless and tendentious wit. Harmless wit gives simple pleasure, tendentious wit a further pleasure, that of aggression and humiliation. In tendentious Freud has made a mistake here; *all* wit is aggressive, even the so-called harmless wit, when closely examined.

Freud also tells us that a joke is the most *social* of all the mental functions that aim at yielding pleasure. A joke, he says, often calls for three persons and the completion of a joke often requires the participation of someone else. Jokes and dreams – he goes on – have grown up in quite different regions of mental life. A dream still remains a wish; a joke is developed play. Dreams retain their connection with the major interests of life; jokes aim at a small yield of pleasure. Dreams serve predominantly for the avoidance of pain or distress; jokes for the attainment of pleasure. But all our mental activity converges on these two aims.

When the poor humorist is determined to *learn* something from a philosopher – to learn how to make a joke – he finds himself in deep waters. He feels like crying and running away.

Koestler in his *Act of Creation* draws two diagrams with zig-zagging lines and explains the whole thing in words: 'The pattern underlying both stories is the perceiving of a situation or idea L, in two self-consistent but habitually incompatible frames of reference, $M_1$ and $M_2$. The event L, in which the two intersect, is made to vibrate simultaneously on two different wave-lengths, as it were. While this situation lasts, L is not merely linked to one associative context, but bisociated with two.'

Am I quoting out of context? Yes. Is this unfair? Certainly. But quoted *in* context, with absolute fairness, it will not come any nearer helping you to make a rattling good joke.

Max Eastman, in the *Enjoyment of Laughter*, draws another terrifying graph which is just as helpful as Koestler's. Koestler, however, raises humour to a new pedestal. According to him the jester is the brother of the scientist and the artist. Comic comparison – humour – is intended to make us laugh; objective analogy – science – to make us understand; poetic image – art – to make us marvel. Creative activity – he goes on to say – is trivalent: it can enter the service of humour, discovery or art. Or put it differently: one branch of the creative activity is humour. The jester is the brother of the sage, perhaps a sage himself. We must be grateful to Koestler for the accolade.

One of the most recent English writers to deal with

this question was Harold Nicolson.* He does not fare any better with definitions than his predecessors. He distinguishes between grim humour, kindly humour, wry humour, pretty humour, sardonic humour, macabre humour and gay humour (using the word in its old sense). But all this is no definition of humour at all. You would not try to define the notion of *hat* by telling us that there are caps, top-hats, bowlers, panamas, bonnets, fezes, helmets, shakos and topees. Undoubtedly there are; but even a longer and more complete list would leave us uninformed as to what a hat is.

But Nicolson tries, in fact, to do a little better than that. He throws together a number of well-known theories on humour, hoping that four theories will tell us more than just one. They do when they complement one another; they tell us less when they contradict one another. He says that there are four theories of laughter (there are, of course, 144 theories of laughter but let us deal with his four). 1. The Theory of Self Esteem. 2. The Theory of Descending Incongruity. 3. The Theory of Release from Constraint and 4. The Theory of Automation as opposed to Free Activity.

The theory of self-esteem is based on Hobbes's famous dictum on 'sudden glory'. It says: '. . . the passion of laughter is nothing else but sudden glory, arising from some sudden conception of some eminency in ourselves, by comparison with the infirmity of others, or with our own formerly.'

One sub-group of this type of laughter is *schadenfreude*, the sheer enjoyment of the misery of others. Nicolson is very proud of the fact that the word *schadenfreude* does not exist in English but I cannot decide whether this proves the nobility of the English character or the poverty of the English language.

---

* *The English Sense of Humour*, by Harold Nicolson, Constable, 1956.

La Rochefoucauld agrees with Hobbes, when he remarks that 'in the misfortunes of our friends there is always something that pleases us.'

Harold Nicolson's second category is 'the descending incongruity' which is Herbert Spencer's phrase. You may wonder what descending incongruity means and when you are told it occurs 'when consciousness is unawares transferred from great things to small', you may go on wondering. It never works the other way round, we are warned. Spencer and Nicolson throw some light on all this: for example, when people make elaborate preparations for fireworks, guests are protected from danger etc, and then there is no glorious and colourful display in the sky, just a faint and feeble sputter, that causes general laughter. When Spencer says that the theory does not work the other way round, he is probably right. When there is a sudden explosion, without any fussy preparations, which kills twenty-seven people and injures another fifty-two, this does not cause general merriment.

Then comes the 'release from constraint'. Boys dismissed from school will enjoy their freedom. With the last point, 'mechanical rigidity', we have already dealt when discussing Bergson. Nicolson's four theories have at least the merit of all-inclusiveness. He takes four well-known and oft-repeated theories and instead of choosing one as the right and only true creed, he throws them together. But even this formidable package tells us very little. Even if his four categories are funny (and they are not) we laugh at many things not included in them.

While we may have learnt a great deal about humour from these eminent thinkers, and have enriched ourselves with most profound ideas, we have still failed to reach a definition. The first Lord Birkenhead, then still F. E. Smith, was once told by a dull and pompous judge: 'Even after your speech, Mr Smith, I am none the wiser.' Smith replied: 'Not wiser, my Lord, but better informed.' This is our position, too. We are much better informed; but not any wiser.

Ferenc Molnár, the great Hungarian playwright and equally great connoisseur of good coffee, once said, after drinking a cup of the suspicious-looking black liquid called coffee which was available in Budapest after the First World War: 'It contains one good thing, one bad thing and a mystery. The good thing is that it contains no chicory; the bad thing is that it contains no coffee. And the mystery is: what makes it black?'

The same with humour. The good thing is that it's amusing; the bad thing is that it's aggressive; the mystery is: what the hell are we really laughing about?

# What Humour *Really* is Not

——◆◦◆◦◆◦◆◦❋◦◆◦◆◦◆◦◆——

PERHAPS YOU WILL SNEER at my statement that – after reading many books on the subject and giving it a great deal of thought – I still have no idea what humour is; and sneer even more when I try to convince any readers that no one else knows what it is, either. You will conclude that I am too slow; too dim. I fail to understand what many others have managed to grasp.

Possibly. I recall an old story which is also about explaining something very difficult to understand. A blind man asks a young girl what milk is.

'Milk?' asks the girl, astonished.

'Yes, milk. You see, I'm blind and I just cannot imagine what milk is like.'

'Well, milk is white.'

'My dear girl,' says the old man, 'I am old and I have been blind all my life. I just don't know what *white* means.'

'Oh, but it's easy to explain,' says the girl helpfully. 'A swan is white.'

'It's easy to say that a swan is white. But I have never seen a swan.'

'It has a curved neck.'

'Curved?' sighs the old man. 'It's easy for you to say "curved". But I have no idea what curved is.'

The girl lifts her arm, bends her wrist forward like a swan's neck.

'Feel it,' she says. 'That's curved.'

The old man feels the girl's arm, touches the curved wrist several times and exclaims joyfully: 'Thank God! Now at last I know what milk is.'

That's it exactly. The same with humour. We know (from Bergson) that it is 'something mechanical encrusted upon the living', that there is an element of inelasticity in it; that it is always corrective and means to humiliate. We also know (from Freud) that sometimes it is and does, sometimes it isn't and doesn't. We know (from Koestler) that the idea L underlies all funny stories in two self-consistent but habitually incompatible frames of reference $M_1$ and $M_2$.

Having read, and absorbed, all this and a lot more, the more intelligent and perceptive among us touch the curved wrists of Bergson, Freud, Koestler, Nicolson, etc, several times and then utter the Eureka-cry: 'Thank God! Now, at last, I know what humour is.'

# Cruel or Kind?

‒◦◉◦◉◦◉◦◉▪❉▪◉◦◉◦◉◦◉◦‒

Now that I have succeeded in muddling my readers with the preliminaries and premises, we can proceed from the general to the particular. Not having understood what humour is, we shall find it much easier to understand what *English Humour* is not. The English are more easygoing about definitions and first principles than the Continentals, and the English are right. They hold with John Stuart Mill that: 'It is no part of the design of this treatise to aim at metaphysical nicety of definition where the ideas suggested by a term are already as determinate as practical purposes require.' Humour is humour, they (and I) say – and go on examining its English subdivision.

Harold Nicolson in his already-mentioned book writes: 'I shall consider whether the sense of humour is in fact an English monopoly and if so whether it is transitory or permanent.'

It is generally assumed (wrongly) that a sense of humour is a purely and exclusively human quality. Only humans have a sense of humour; and all humans have some sort of a sense of humour. So make no mistake: the question that Nicolson asks here is whether the English are the only members of the human race on earth *and if so* why are aliens so inhuman?

The result of his exploration, not surprisingly, is that yes, only the English are human, although he does not quite say it in so many words. What he says is this: 'Englishmen regard their sense of humour as cosy,

comfortable, contemplative, lazy and good-humoured.'
How a sense of humour can be good-humoured and lazy
are questions on which we need not dwell. But to me the
English sense of humour also looks cruel, not particularly witty, childish and often vicious. Such things have
been said before and they puzzled Nicolson. How is it –
he asks – that to foreigners the English sense of humour
seems to be atrabilious and dour?

Taine (quoted by Nicolson) remarked more than a
century ago: 'The man who jests in England is seldom
kindly and never happy.' Indeed, Englishmen have
always been fond – and proud – of saying that they take
their pleasures sadly. Taine added: 'For people of another
race [English humour] is disagreeable; our nerves find it
too sharp and bitter.'

This hardly fits in with Nicolson's view of the English
character. The English national characteristics are,
according to him: good humour, tolerance, ready sympathy, compassion; an affection for nature, animals,
children; a fund of common sense; a wide and generous
gift for fancy; a respect for individual character rather
than for individual intelligence; a dislike of extremes, of
overemphasis and boastfulness; a love of games; diffi-
dence; shyness; laziness; optimism.

This self-portrait of the English does not reflect a dislike of boastfulness – but the English know how to boast
modestly. A lot of what Nicolson says is true, of course,
but what about a few other traits of English character?
Cruelty? Conceit? Snobbery? An incurable feeling of
superiority? Dislike of everything foreign and strange? A
stick-in-the-mud traditionalism and abhorrence of everything new?

Humour – like beauty – is in the beholder's eye. But
the beholder's eye is determined by the beholder's character, so we might as well have a quick look at some
relevant aspects of the English character.

# Changing or Permanent?

WHEN I FIRST came to England I was struck by the English: their outlook on life, their humour, their phlegm, their affected and real superiority, their insularity and their aloofness from the rest of the human race. Their impact on me was overwhelming. I have lived through exciting times, like everybody else of my generation, but the most important, most formative and most significant event in my life was my emigration: to be transplanted from the coffee-houses of Budapest to the cricket grounds of England is a shocking experience for a man who knows how to drink coffee but has no idea how to play cricket.

I described my impression of the English in an early book called *How to be an Alien*, which most people regarded as humorous although it was in fact a desperate *cri de cœur*, a forlorn cry for help. Because my first impression was so overwhelming, the picture in my mind does not change easily. Yet I have to ask myself: is England still the same country which I set foot on (and which set foot on me) in 1938? Has the English character changed out of recognition (as many people say) or is it permanent and unchangeable (as others maintain)? If it *has* changed, in what way?

National character does not change with the rapidity of the weather. You cannot say that the British national character was sunny in the second half of September,

1938, and cloudy and turbulent in the first week of April, 1980. But you can observe tendencies, note changes and recognize trends.

National character, like individual character, is partly inherited, partly formed by the environment. Whether one or the other plays a greater part in character formation, and what the exact ratio is, need not concern us here. As the circumstances – the environment – of the British have changed since the war, the national character has also changed. The three cardinal events of the last forty years in the history of Britain were: the winning of the war, the loss of the Empire and the shift in the power structure in British society.

What has been the effect of these events? Was it beneficial or detrimental? The answer to the second question is: both. Under stress, good people become better, bad people become worse.

The winning of the war left the least impression on the British character. They were used to winning wars. They knew it had been touch and go – as on many occasions before – but muddling through was very much in the British line and they were also used to being lucky. At the end of the war they realized – it was not difficult – that the United States and the Soviet Union were much greater powers but Britain was still a leading world power enjoying good-will and influence, a permanent member of the Security Council, the centre of a great Empire and enjoying tremendous prestige.

The loss of the Empire was a different matter and a great shock. Britain ceased to be a world power, one of the top nations, the supreme arbiter. The rest of the world was not there just to keep her in luxury. There were two basic reactions to this event. One group was ready to face realities and indeed even unrealities, since enjoying disasters and gloom is a good old British habit. Britain, according to them, was now about as important as Portugal – another former Imperial power. This group kept making jokes about losing India but keeping Gibraltar. They were altogether much too self-effacing and self-belittling. The other group acted as if nothing had happened. After all, it was not the Empire that made Britain; Britain made the Empire. For them Britain has remained all-powerful, the top nation, just because the British are the British – magnificent, inimitable, quaint. Palmerston is still Foreign Secretary, recalcitrant European tribal chiefs ought to be birched. The poorer the country became, the deeper it sank into the economic morass, the louder these people have beaten their chests, the more xenophobic, racist, conceited, class-conscious, snobbish and insular they have become.

The third great change, the shift in the power structure, affects the national character in two ways. If I may quote myself, I have said somewhere else: Britain is the society where the ruling class does not rule, the working class does not work and the middle class is not in the middle. Social classes are on the move and classes on the move are always bloody awful: desperate, bitter and paranoid if they move downwards, power-hungry, gloating, revengeful and self-conscious if they move upwards. A lot can be said against a hereditary aristocracy in a stable society but at least they are secure, self-confident and believe in themselves, however unjustified such a belief may be.

The second trouble is that the British working class is probably the least well-educated in Western Europe. I was struck by this fact when I first came here and still cannot get over it. Trade union experts told me then that education was a long-term affair; but forty years is a long term and a lot could have been achieved between then and now. Then they were engaged in gaining the next 'substantial rise' in wages; they are engaged in the same battle today. The British working class has, of course, a

*'Classes on the move are always bloody awful.'*

great deal of natural intelligence but the best brains opt out and forget their working-class origins (except in their memoirs where it makes good reading) and the second eleven become trade union leaders and lead their battalions from behind, according to rules and principles learnt during the thirties. The state of education is probably worse today than it was forty years ago and when you see the general level of working-class people in, say, Sweden or Germany and think of our own, you want to weep at the ignorance and backwardness of ours. The result is that there are a million and a half unemployed in Britain yet, at one and the same time, a tremendous shortage of highly skilled engineers, designers etc. Masses of British workers are just too uneducated and ignorant to take these jobs. I am not mixing up frills with education: they are too uneducated to acquire the necessary skills. This is not their failure; it is the failure of successive governments and above all the failure of the trade unions.

The public-school manner which was prevalent in British society for so long is being slowly eroded. It is no longer fashionable to have the manners of an ageing adolescent, to suppress all emotions, to admire 'character' and despise intellect; and the vague idea that 'fairness' is the supreme law of society is in decline. But the stiff upper lip still rules. At the time of writing there are regular twice-weekly railway strikes in England, a lorry-drivers' strike, a municipal workers' strike, a civil-servants' strike and a miners' strike are threatening, there are shortages of food and other articles in the shops, the number of unemployed is growing every hour and on top of it all the country is snowed under, many roads are impassable and the airports are closed. In many other countries there would be revolution or civil war. Here the Home Secretary keeps telling the House that there is no crisis, the House nods – with the exception of a few Opposition members who smile ironically. The general public does not bother much about these little local difficulties. They shrug their shoulders and get on with their jobs – not too enthusiastically, but no less diligently than on other occasions.

In the past the supreme moral code of the British was fairness. Shoplifting and murder could be forgiven; queue-jumping not. You could call the British stupid (indeed, they were offended if you called them clever) but you could not call them unfair. British bank-robbers and safe-breakers pleaded guilty and went to prison; but once there they would stab a fellow-prisoner in the back with a long, sharp knife if he had called them unfair. Those days are over. Fairness is now regarded by an increasing number of people as silly sentimentality. Who *wants* to be fair?

It was pointed out to a trade union official during the lorry-drivers' strike that he was cutting off food-supplies to ordinary people with whom he has no dispute whatsoever. He replied: 'If I can't eat why should they?' The leader of the ambulancemen declared on the eve of *their* strike that they would not answer even emergency calls and added: 'And if it means lives lost, that's how it must be.'

This is not the mentality, the tone which people used to associate with England. This is not the old British character; it is the new one. The shining British virtues were the virtues of superiority, self-confidence and well-being; they are being replaced by the vices of inferiority, insecurity and poverty. Kindness and tolerance are on the way out; indifference and meanness are on the way in. The great virtues are not gone completely, far from it, but they do shine much less dazzlingly than they did even in the recent past.

# Three Faces of English Humour

<hr/>

THE ENGLISH sense of humour has three characteristics which distinguish it from others. Or to be more precise: other peoples have one or another of these characteristics (Jewish humour, for instance, is just as self-mocking as the English), but only the English have the three together and it is not so much the three individual traits as the chemistry of the three together which creates something unique.

## Laughing at Yourself

If a sense of humour were simply the ability to laugh, everybody would have a sense of humour. Stalin was not one of the great humorous characters of our age but even he was able to laugh until tears flowed down his cheeks. Milovan Djilas describes a blood-chilling scene at one of those notorious dinner-parties which on the one hand amused the participants and, on the other, decided the fate of the Soviet Union and Eastern Europe. They were discussing the execution of Zinoviev. Beria – another man who is not exactly remembered for his uproarious comic turns – began imitating Zinoviev's agony in the last minutes of his life. The joke lay in Zinoviev's terror, and

Beria imitated his shrieks, cries, moans and frantic appeals to Stalin who – Zinoviev supposed – was ignorant of his being murdered. Zinoviev was a Jew and to add to the merriment Beria put on a Jewish accent. Stalin was roaring with laughter, his face became red, tears were running down his cheeks and he asked Beria to repeat the performance. A solicitous Molotov, however, stopped the repeat performance half-way through, being anxious that too much laughter might harm Stalin's delicate health.

I also remember a lovely Irish girl who told me: 'My girlfriend and I have such a wonderful sense of humour. We just sit down and laugh and laugh for hours for no reason whatsoever.'

All this, from Stalin to little Deirdre, may pass for a sense of humour. But a sense of humour, I believe, really begins when one is able to laugh at oneself. That's where a sense of proportion – something useful and positive – comes in. The person who can laugh at himself sees himself (more or less) as others see him. He can smile at his own misfortune, folly and weakness. He may even be able to accept the idea that in a disagreement the other person, too, may have a point.

Humorists discovered the advantages of such an attitude long ago. The humorous piece in which the writer describes himself as clumsy, foolish, gullible and incompetent is a very old device. The reason behind this is twofold: 1) some humorists – give credit where credit is due – do, after all, possess a genuine sense of humour and are capable of laughing at themselves; 2) they play the clown because they know that the world loves a clown more than it loves a humorist.

The humorist, as a rule, is a satirist, a purifier, a moralist. Although he wears an apologetic smile, he wants to chastise and purify us. The clown is a very special figure and touches deep chords at the bottom of our hearts.* The clown is a depreciated father-figure, a man of authority deprived of his standing. He looks grand and is often cruel, like Father he tries to make us believe that he knows everything, that he can do everything, but in fact, he is only a fool, no better than us. Like Father, he wants us to think him big and alarming, but he is not: he is feeble, ridiculous, incompetent and just as much lost in this world as the rest of us. We are delighted to discover this, we are relieved and revel in our sudden glory: but the clown is essentially a sad and melancholy figure. Every time he fights a windmill, he suffers defeat; time and again he runs his head against a brick wall only to discover that the wall is hard and his head is soft. And – saddest of all – he realizes that he cannot really protect those whom he is called upon to protect.

Yet there is a further essential relationship with the clown: we love him. He is Father; we want to see him humbled, ridiculed, brought down to our lowly level, but we still love him. To hate Father would generate guilt in us and we could not enjoy his humiliation; we cannot laugh at the clown with an entirely clear conscience.

So when the humorist starts clowning he doesn't just simply make fun of himself; he uses a device to gain our hearts.

The first person singular also increases the dramatic effect of the story. 'A funny thing happened to me on the way to the Forum . . .' is an age-old trick. Why is it, people often ask, that funny things keep happening to humorists and nothing funny ever happens to them? The truth is that funny things do keep happening to them. The majority of the funny things described by humorists in the first person singular happened to their friends,

* See a more detailed reasoning on this in my book *Humour in Memoriam*, Routledge & Kegan Paul and André Deutsch, 1970.

bank managers, business connections, who never noticed them. Indeed, the only essential difference between the ordinary person and the humorist is that the latter notices the humour in situations where the others miss it.

It was G. K. Chesterton who gave the perfect – and to my mind, final – answer to the question when he remarked, speaking of humanity at large: 'You make the jokes: I see them.'

Leaving literary conventions and devices apart, the English have the gift – a very precious one – of being able to laugh at themselves and their own weaknesses. The first step any foreign students of English humour, trying to acquire it, must take is to accept the idea that they are not perfect; that in some cases they may be wrong; that they are not, at one and the same time, beautiful, omniscient, accomplished sportsmen and generous souls. They must reconcile themselves to the idea that their profile is not Roman and their handwriting is a mess. The English, at least, suspect as much.

Not very long ago one of the great wits and most popular after-dinner speakers of London was a judge, Lord Birkett. He was giving one of his after-dinner speeches, when he suddenly interrupted himself, looked at a man across the table and said: 'I don't mind someone looking at his watch when I speak; but I object when somebody puts his watch to his ear, because he can hardly believe that it is going.'

In the early years when the British car industry was in the doldrums, I went to see the Motor Car Exhibition. The Rolls-Royce stand was derelict, the man in charge – in striped trousers, black jacket, grey tie and small, saucy, military moustache – seemed lonely and forlorn. A ragged man, a prowler, in shabby overcoat and with a two-day beard came up to him and asked: 'Where's the gentlemen's toilet, Guv'nor?'

The Rolls-Royce salesman jumped off his stand:

*'First genuine enquiry I've had for three days.'*

'Permit me to guide you there, sir,' he replied and conducted the man to the loo. When he returned, the salesman from the next stand, representing a much more modest make, asked him: 'Are you mad? Why did you do that?'

The Rolls-Royce chap explained: 'That was the first genuine enquiry I've had for three days.'

The same kind of self-deprecation and self-mockery on a national level is exemplified in a joke popular at a time of economic crisis, when – on top of everything else – Britain and the world were threatened with yet another oil-price rise.

His secretary rushes in to the Chancellor of the Exchequer and tells him, breathless with excitement: 'Chancellor . . . something terrible has happened . . . The Pope and Sheikh Yamani . . . you know, the Oil Minister of Saudi Arabia – have arrived together. They both want to see you without delay. Whom should I let in first?'

The Chancellor thinks a bit, then replies: 'Send in the Pope. With the Pope I have to kiss only his ring.'

A subdivision of this attitude, this state of mind is the 'sorry, my fault' business. It has become a major industry in Britain (now in decline, like all major industries). It is a product of the public-school code: acknowledge your shortcomings and mistakes, face your responsibilities. So far so good; but it has been degraded over the years, it has become a facile phrase, the easy way out. If any aspiring foreigner wants to get on here, this is the first phrase he must learn. Never mind whose mistake it is, when you come out with the magic 'Sorry, my fault,' the English are disarmed. What can they say to such a decent chap who accepts responsibility? The phrase used to mean: 'Forgive me, I have made a mistake.' Nowadays it means: 'Who cares what's really happened. Let's shut up, forget about it and concentrate on something less boring.'

The big question about self-mockery is this: are the British really laughing at their faults or are they laughing only at those of their faults which they regard as gentlemanly and endearing? The one other people who laugh at themselves as readily as the English, are the Jews. They do laugh at their *real* shortcomings readily, perhaps too readily. (More of Jewish humour later.) About the English Harold Nicolson remarked: 'The Englishman will often relish jokes directed against those of his failings (such as absent-mindedness, greediness, unpunctuality, untidiness, extravagance) which do not diminish his essential dignity, he will never laugh at jokes directed against failings of which he is inwardly ashamed.'

I go further. A great deal of inverted snobbery is attached to these acceptable, likeable, elegant faults. I think it would be quite appropriate to recall an evening I described in the fifties:

I was invited to a rather dull party. Conversation sagged and there was general boredom in the air. One of the guests – I had never seen him before – told me that he owned large shops.

'Good for you,' I replied.

'Not one shop,' he added, 'but several.'

'Yes, I've got the point,' I nodded. As he went on telling me about his various shops, I asked him where his headquarters were.

'In Cricklewood,' he said.

Up to that moment he had been just as bored with our conversation as I was myself. But suddenly a light appeared in his eye.

'I don't know that district at all,' he said. 'Do you?'

'Yes, I know it very well,' I replied.

'I don't,' he insisted. 'I've been there for thirty years but I still don't know that district at all.'

He was becoming agitated and I saw from the

expression in his eyes that I was not supposed to think: 'How stupid!' but to look at him with admiration and wonder.

'There are two streets in my immediate neighbourhood,' he continued, 'one is called Exeter Road, the other Exeter Parade.'

'Yes,' I said, 'there are.'

'Do you know them?' he asked me.

'I know them both very well,' I replied.

'Well, I don't,' he said triumphantly. 'I have been there for thirty years and I still don't know which is Exeter Road and which is Exeter Parade.'

He looked around, pleased with himself beyond measure. It was no minor achievement. He seemed to imply: 'Only an exceptionally able, shrewd and brilliant man can be quite as stupid as that.'

'Actually,' he went on, 'it's thirty-two years, not thirty – and I *still* don't know one from the other.'

So I explained it to him. I explained with great care which was Exeter Road and which was Exeter Parade. He looked at me with bewilderment. So did all the others. What a bore I was; what a spoil-sport. Did I want to take away this man's only claim to fame? Quite frankly, I did.

But it was too late. The others paid no attention to me. The man's remarks had enlivened the conversation and the party came to life; everybody was eager to have his turn. Everyone told us how utterly silly he was. One story was capped by another. One man knew the names of the streets in his district all right, but had such a bad sense of direction that he kept losing his way even in the immediate neighbourhood of his house. Whenever he wanted to make a short cut he was sure to land miles away. Another man said that he was unable to remember names. A couple of others said they knew what he meant, they could never remember names either, whereupon he insisted, rather ferociously, that no one could possibly be quite so bad on names as he was. He looked round defiantly and no one dared challenge him. A fourth person boasted that he could not remember faces and a fifth that he was incapable of mending fuses. We lingered over the topic of mechanical imbecility but this contest was easily won by a lady who alleged that she was unable even to wind up her watch. Then the man who owned so many shops butted in to say again that although he had been working in Cricklewood for thirty years – thirty-two, to be precise – he still could not tell Exeter Road from Exeter Parade.

So they went on confessing to faults and failings which – needless to say – they did not regard as faults and failings at all. All this self-deprecation meant only: how wonderful we must be if we can afford to admit so much against ourselves. Or else: if we have to be stupid, then – by God – we're going to be the stupidest people in the world. We want to excel *somehow*.

### Understatement

Understatement is not a trick, not a literary device: it is a way of life. It is a *weltanschauung*, i.e. a way of looking at the world. You have to breathe the air of England, live with these understanding, tolerant – some say sheepish – people for a while before you get it into your blood. Unless you learn what understatement is you have not made even the first step towards understanding English humour. Life is one degree under in England and so is every manifestation of life.

A lawyer is working in his study on a hard case when a workman – who has to do some repairs in the house – crosses the room. The lawyer exclaims: 'How can I be expected to do any work when armies of workmen keep marching up and down in front of my nose?' This lawyer is not an English lawyer – neither a barrister, nor a solicitor. A man sneezes in a pub and another tells him: 'If you've got the cholera why don't you stay at home?' This is not an Englishman and not an English pub.

These are both wild overstatements. Many people try to achieve, and often succeed in achieving, humorous effects this way. But it is not the English way. Take the English passion for queueing. As some people need occasional outbursts of temper – an Italian will feel much relieved after smashing a few plates or after having a flaming row with somebody on any subject – so an Englishman needs an occasional outburst of discipline and self-control. This need probably stems from the old virtues of tolerance, courtesy, self-assurance; they are changing perhaps, and fading away slowly, but they have not disappeared yet – far from it.

Understatement is also underreaction. P. G. Wodehouse's Bertie Wooster speaks to his valet:

'Have you seen Mr Fink-Nottle, Jeeves?'

'No, sir.'

'I am going to murder him.'

'Very good, sir.'

When gales are raging, trees are torn up and houses are blown away like cardboard, an Englishman will remark: 'Rather windy, isn't it?' When it rains cats and dogs, or there is hail and sleet plus freezing fog, an Englishman, meeting his neighbour on his way to the local railway-station, will comment: 'Not a very nice day, is it?' If someone expresses his views with vehemence, passion and dogmatic fervour, an Englishman may tell him: 'You really think so?' In a more temperamental Continental country this would be worded slightly differently: 'You are talking utter rot and it is beneath my dignity to go on talking with such a fool as you.' But the meaning of the two statements is exactly the same.

The whole rhythm of life in England is understatement;

their suppression of emotion is understatement; their underreaction to everything, the polite word instead of the expletive (when the latter would help so much more to clear the air), the stiff upper lip, the very climate with its absence of extremes, all these are understatement.

The London *Evening Standard* reported one day that Concorde had resumed its London–Bahrain service on a twice-weekly basis but had left Heathrow without one single passenger. When a British Airways spokesman was asked about this somewhat curious state of affairs, he replied: 'We never expected the service to be overcrowded.'

There is no other country in the world where this reply could have been made. The story comes from 'This England', a weekly feature in the *New Statesman & Nation*. They publish authentic extracts from the British press and recently they collected three years' crop in a booklet.

Or – speaking of understatement – take one or two examples of English patience and tolerance. Pauline Jenkins (writes the *News of the World*) had a 'hell of a shock' when she discovered on her wedding night that her husband was a woman. She told a reporter later: 'I threatened to leave then and there.' But later she calmed down, went down to the kitchen and 'had a cup of tea *instead*'.

A violent English family scene as reported by *The Times*: Mrs Diana Evans, mother of three children and married for seventeen years, called to her husband in the garden. 'I am getting a divorce.' The news was shattering; utterly unexpected; the husband's marriage lay in ruins. His answer was: 'If I do not get these tomato plants in soon they will die.'

The English equivalent of the *crime passionel*, quoted from the *Lymington Times*: a husband, incensed when he found his wife in bed with another man, drew a huge and murderous knife and thrust it into the heart of their daughter's teddy-bear.

Or, again, look at the manner in which a true Englishman faces death. The *Southend Standard* reported that Mr Victor Shaw, a dustman, having emptied the dustbins at a caravan-site at Rochdale, found a mortar bomb in one. The bomb proved to be live and nearly blew the dust-cart with Mr Shaw and his whole gang in it to smithereens. Mr Shaw's comment was that he wished, when people threw bombs into the dustbin, that they would indicate on a small bit of paper whether the bombs were live or not.

There are Sunday Trading Laws in force in England. Flowers and food – being perishable goods – may be sold on Sundays but other goods may be sold only in open markets by Jews (or Moslems) who keep their Sabbaths on Saturdays (or Fridays). No one takes much notice of these laws but Croydon Council decided that they were to be enforced with greater strictness. The flower and food dealers shrugged their shoulders, they were not affected. But what about the other eighty-two stallholders? The plan to close their market would have created a riot in some more temperamental Southern countries; four hundred years ago the Inquisition might have stepped in; seven hundred years ago it might have proved the *casus belli* for a religious war. But in England, Anno Domini 1978, the eighty-two stallholders – good Christians to a man – found another solution. They all declared that they were Jews and went on trading.

*Cruelty*

British humour has a strong streak of cruelty.

It is amazing that these seemingly gentle people deem certain things funny which horrify others. What is the explanation? That these gentle people are not so gentle, after all? That the rest of the world is too squeamish? Or perhaps something more subtle and complicated?

The first objection to this statement – that British humour is cruel – is the simple reply that *all* humour is cruel. The idea that humour is gentle and sweet and that the humorist, or even the man with a good sense of humour, is a nice and likeable chap is nonsense. Humour is always aggressive. On the lowest level we laugh, or at least giggle nervously, at the man who has slipped on one of those famous banana skins. Our 'sudden glory' is always connected with someone else's sudden discomfiture or ignominy.*

'Wit is related to aggression, hostility and sadism. Humour is related to depression, narcissism and masochism' – to quote Dr Martin Grotjahn's *Beyond Laughter*. Dr Grotjahn goes over a number of manifestations of humour. He starts with 'kidding'. Kidding is an American expression but needs no explanation in Britain either. Kidding means to treat someone like a kid, in other words to assume a superior, pseudo-authoritarian attitude towards him. 'The inveterate kidder,' writes Dr Grotjahn, 'expresses his own conflict with authority (usually his parents) and projects it onto his victim. The kidder imitates his father torturing his "kid" who is in a position of humiliation and passive endurance ... He can dish it out but he cannot take it.' After the kidder comes the practical joker. He is the eternal adolescent, his aggression is barely disguised. My brother is a mild and compassionate man but with an occasionally explosive temperament. He used to be fond of mild practical jokes, but even these were cruel, or at least aggressive. For example, if you had a bad cold my brother, in his young days, was liable to wait for you to feel a sneeze coming on – then he would jerk your handkerchief away so that you were caught in mid-sneeze and either sneezed

---

* The same subject is treated at greater length in my book *Humour in Memoriam*, Routledge & Kegan Paul and André Deutsch, 1970.

into your own hand or choked. Not a joke to please sensitive and susceptible souls. My brother would also stop someone in the street and ask him if he knew where, say, Bedford Avenue was. The victim would say, sorry, he didn't know. Then my brother would explain to him, with all decorum, that it was second on the right, then first on the left.

The second joke is just mildly aggressive, the first has an element of cruelty in it. The well-known joke that follows (not my brother's) aims at humiliating the victim. A man is invited to a nudist party and arrives full of expectations. The butler – one of the conspirators – receives him with deferential courtesy, takes him to a side-room and tells him to undress. When stark naked, he is ceremoniously announced and enters a room where everyone else is properly dressed in evening gowns and dinner jackets, complete with jewels and decorations.

The rule is that the victim of this sort of adolescent sadism has to accept the joke good-humouredly, otherwise he is regarded as a bore, with no sense of humour. If he loses his temper, he becomes even more ridiculous. The only accepted way of retaliation or revenge is by means of another, even crueller, practical joke.

Now consider a few examples of verbal wit. W. S. Gilbert, many years after Wagner's death, was asked at a party by a lady with high-brow pretensions: 'Tell me, Mr Gilbert, is dear old Richard Wagner still composing?' 'No, Madam,' replied Gilbert, 'actually he is decomposing.'

Then there is the famous quip: 'Psychoanalysis is the disease it pretends to cure,' or Wilde's celebrated remarks about a famous novelist: 'Ah, Meredith! Who can define him? His style is chaos illuminated by flashes of lightning. As a writer he has mastered everything, except language; as a novelist he can do everything, except tell a story.' Or Wilde again, having been informed that Osgood, the go-ahead publisher who advertised the fact that all his

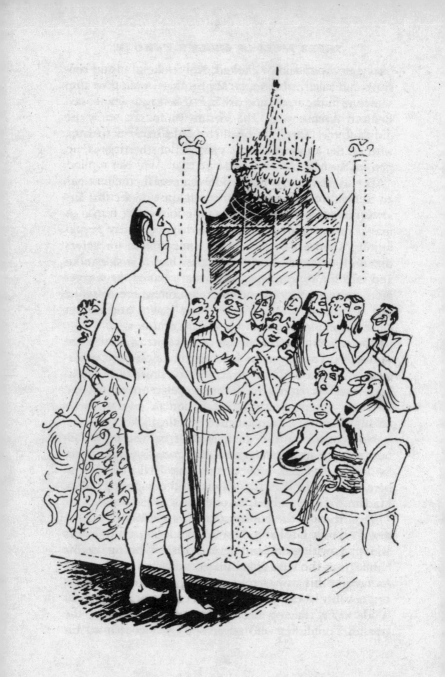

books were published simultaneously in London and New York, had died. 'He is a great loss to us. I suppose they will bury him simultaneously in London and New York.'

Each of these witticisms fills us with the desire: 'I wish I'd said it.' (Even Wilde felt this irresistible desire and once, when applauding one of Whistler's witticisms, he, too, exclaimed: 'I wish I had said that.' Whistler replied: 'You will, Oscar, you will.') But whatever their charm, all of them are offensive, aimed against a victim and designed to establish the wit's superiority over him.

Wit comes easily, even compulsively – to many people. It can become a way of life in some circles, in literary groups, in Central European cafés. It is *bellum omnium contra omnes*, very much with the survival of the fittest. The wit's aim is murder. Everyone is fair game. The witticism is a thinly disguised insult, you can either retaliate on the same level or you have to grin as if you enjoyed it. But when this ruthless blood-sport is confined within a particular set of people it is not altogether unfair. Members of the circle know what to expect and, in any case, the jokes soon become repetitive, follow a pattern and become boring – although the players cannot desist; it is their way of life. The whole thing becomes altogether cruel (and usually more amusing in its horror) when the hunter happens on an outsider, an innocent and completely unprepared victim, who becomes embarrassed, has no idea how to take it and is inclined to break down in tears.

'The wit . . . is hostile, often with a skilful, artful, highly developed, sophisticated meanness and viciousness,' says Dr Grotjahn, and he compares him to a man who plays with sparks but never lights a warming fire. He thinks that the wit's irresistible tendency to make witty remarks 'is his way of releasing his hostility. Without it, he probably would blow his top or get a migraine attack.'

The cynic is a special type of wit: he is not just a 'distressing fault-finder' as one dictionary defines him. The

*Shorter Oxford Dictionary* is much better: The cynic 'is one disposed to decry and sneer at the sincerity or goodness of human motives or actions'. This refusal to believe in human goodness is an essential factor in the cynic – whose name, by the way, comes from an ancient school of philosophy which took it, in turn, from the Greek word for 'dog' (*kuon*) because of their manners. The cynic either pulls down something lofty and noble to an every-day level, or sees the mean motive behind the noble act.

A favourite slogan of German propaganda in two World Wars: 'The British will fight to the last gasp of the last Frenchman.' Or Wilde: 'If a man is too unimaginative to produce evidence in support of a lie, he might as well speak the truth at once.' An oft-heard comment on the United States: 'What a great country God could make the United States – if only he had the money.' Or Wilde again, on the infinite goodness of the Almighty: 'Don't you realize that missionaries are the divinely provided food of cannibals? Whenever they are on the brink of starvation, heaven, in its infinite mercy, sends them a nice, plump missionary.' The cynic makes fun of death; or he jokes about the downright horrible. Cynicism keeps tears away, which is why soldiers joke about impending battles, or ambulance men – otherwise not given to cynicism – about road casualties. Medical students joke during anatomy lessons, surrounded by corpses and dismembered limbs.

Jokes about death and horror all tend to show that the cynic is tough; that he can take it; that he is not afraid of things that worry the rest of us. But, of course, he is even more afraid; he is permanently preoccupied with the fear that he is joking about. Cynicism always has an element of cowardice in it. It is rarely the convinced atheist who tells cynical jokes about God or calls him by insulting names, but the agnostic who is afraid that God may, after all, exist and punish him. It is always the man who is afraid of, or preoccupied with, death who jokes about it. The cynical joke is an attempt to tame a powerful opponent. The cynic tries to get on familiar terms with Death, or God, or Cancer, tries to make Death his chum, just a chap standing around the bar enjoying half a bitter in his company, an amiable fellow, Death; surely, he will not harm *me*? This is one way of taming death, of making it look less frightful.

Cynical remarks, naturally enough, often hurt people. Religious people (particularly if deep down in their hearts they have doubts) resent dirty jokes about God; devoted monarchists (especially when they feel some lingering uneasiness lest the Queen be, after all, just an ordinary human being) resent jokes about the Sovereign, etc. Everybody has a borderline beyond which he will cease to see the joke and will protest and walk out in disgust. No one likes to do this, as the cynic is accepted as a sophisticated person and he will always try to show up the critic who resents his jokes as an unsophisticated boor. Yet there is a limit to everybody's tolerance.

Satire, too, is aggressive, a way of humiliating others and establishing the satirist's superiority. Even if the satirist does not state that he could do better, sitting in judgement on others always implies superiority. But here another element must also be taken into consideration: *who and what are the targets of satire?*

The satirist is often a journalist or pamphleteer whose only weapon is his pen with which he fights kings, tyrants and obnoxious political regimes. Whether we agree with him or not, he deserves our admiration because of his courage. But what about the *Stuermer*, a German satirical weekly? The *Stuermer*'s butt was the Jews, who were then being sent to the gas ovens. And in Russia newspaper satirists used to do a lot of jeering at the Kulaks who were being executed in their millions (a kulak in those days was any person disliked by the regime). I once heard (indirectly) some jokes a hangman had told about men he had hanged.

When we talk about *sneering*, *sarcasm* and *jeering*, we do not really mean that the joke, as a joke, is bad but only that it outrages our moral instinct so much that we refuse to examine its power to amuse. A *sneer* or a *jeer* is a satirical joke we disagree with; satire or irony is the type of *jeering* and *sneer* we approve of.

Satire, in addition to its aggressive content, has a strong moral content, and no decent and civilized man can laugh at jokes aimed at people who cannot hit back. The satirist who hits at the mighty and powerful is a hero; the satirist who hits at the man who is down, is a cad.

Humour is aggressive and always aggressive. There is no such thing as non-aggressive humour. Nonsense! you may reply. What about sex jokes, for example? Obscene jokes are a form of sexual aggression. Sometimes the most aggressively worded jokes contain more understanding, even affection, than the seemingly milder ones, yet they remain aggressive. (A woman was dug out of the ruins of her house during the blitz of London, having spent hours in the debris. Someone asked her: 'Where's your husband?' She replied: 'Fighting in Libya – the bloody coward.') Perhaps it is nonsense jokes which seem to come nearest to being non-aggressive. Two chaps meet. One says to the other: 'Didn't we meet in Newcastle, years ago?' The other shakes his head: 'Never been to Newcastle in my life.' 'Neither have I,' says the first chap and then adds reflectively: 'Must have been two other fellows.' Who is the butt of this joke? – one may ask. The first chap? The second? Well, who? Nonsense humour is more purely aggressive than that: it is an act of rebellion against reason, against the established order. Thus nonsense humour, with its modest and charming smile, is more aggressive, indeed destructive, than any other kind of humour.

We might as well add to all this that the kidder, the teaser, the wit, the cynic, the satirist and even to some extent the practitioner of the sneer and the jeer, are all trying to find a *permissible outlet* for their aggression.

Aggressiveness in humour is a general phenomenon; cruelty in humour is more specifically English. What's the difference between aggressiveness and cruelty? The aggressive man *wants* to hurt, often for good or at least subjectively valid reasons; the cruel man is indifferent to the suffering of others – or else takes special delight in it.

Peasant humour or childish humour is cruel everywhere. I once told a story to my son, when he was very young, which I made up as I went on. We – he and I – were caught by Red Indians who threatened to eat us up. The cauldrons were already prepared and the water boiling when, quite unexpectedly and in the nick of time, we were rescued. When I finished, my son said: 'Now tell me that story again, but in the end they should save only me and the Red Indians should eat you up.' At a certain level of culture and sophistication – or growing up – cruelty fades out in most of us. But not in England. English humour may be, and often is, witty and erudite, yet it revels in cruelty.

The first nursery rhyme British children learn is about Humpty-Dumpty who sat on a wall, had a great fall and the result is that all the king's horses and all the king's men will not put Humpty-Dumpty together again. I do not suggest that Humpty-Dumpty and similar nursery rhymes turn children into bloodthirsty monsters; all I say is that English children start to learn laughing at great falls and disasters at an early age.

One of the most often quoted examples of English literary cruelty is Swift's *Modest Proposal*. But Swift was not English – in fact, according to Stephen Potter he was extremely un-English – and the piece is not cruel at all.

There are too many beggar boys in Ireland, says Swift, and it would be desirable to find a fair, cheap and easy method of making these children sound and useful members of the commonwealth. And why stick to children of beggars when there are too many poor children in the kingdom, everywhere? Swift's solution is a simple one: 'I have been assured by a very knowing *American* of my acquaintance in *London* that a young, healthy *Child* well Nursed is at a year Old a most delicious, nourishing, and wholesome Food, whether *Stewed*, *Roasted*, *Baked or Boyled* and I make no doubt that it will equally serve in a *Fricasce*, or a *Ragoust*.'

He goes on in this vein. '. . . the remaining hundred thousand [children] may at a year Old be offered in sale to *persons* of Quality, and *Fortune*, through the Kingdom, always advising the Mother to let them Suck plentifully in the last Month, so as to render them Plump and Fat for a good Table. A Child will make two Dishes at an Entertainment for Friends, and when the Family dines alone, the fore or the hind Quarter will make a reasonable Dish, and seasoned with a little Pepper or Salt will be very good Boiled on the fourth Day, especially in Winter.'

This is not cruelty but very good satire. His red-hot anger and ice-cold contempt for a society which condemns children to death through poverty comes clearly through.

'I Profess in the sincerity of my Heart that I have not the least personal interest in endeavouring to promote this necessary work having no other Motive than the *publick Good of my Country*, by *advancing our Trade, providing for Infants, relieving the Poor, and giving some Pleasure to the Rich*. I have no Children, by which I can propose to get a single Penny; the youngest being nine Years old, and my wife past Childbearing.'

Edward Lear is one of my great favourites. Harold Nicolson writes about him: 'The mortality among Lear's characters, although fortunately the majority of them were of foreign origin, is high. A girl of Smyrna is burnt to death (or almost burnt to death) by her own grandmother; a Norwegian girl is crushed in a door; a Czechoslovak citizen* contracts the plague; a Peruvian is thrust into a stove by his wife and a similar fate overcomes a Prussian; an inhabitant of Cromer falls off a cliff and a citizen of Calcutta is choked to death; an unnamed oriental dies of remorse observing the gluttony of his children; a maiden at Janina has her head blown off; an old lady at Stroud commits mass murder; and two citizens, respectively of Ems and Cadiz meet their death by drowning.'

W. S. Gilbert is another writer I love and admire. Often, in many operettas, he laughs at old age and feebleness; torture, executions, beating and boiling people in oil are sources of constant merriment. Just a few examples: *The Mikado* is full of these jocular references to death, execution and torture. The hero is the Lord High Executioner, the Mikado himself sings his justly famous and witty song about his determination 'to let the punishment fit the crime'. All this is harmless enough but even that song contains lines like this:

> It is my very humane endeavour
> To make to some extent,
> Each evil liver
> A running river
> Of harmless merriment.

I know it is 'all a joke' but people's jokes are revealing. Dostoevsky, Kafka, Koestler and Solzhenitsyn have described incomparably greater horrors than the Mikado but the reader never feels that they are on the side of the torturers, that they laugh *with* the executioners at their victims and that they regard these matters as harmless merriment. One can say, of course, that Gilbert in fact

* Extremely unlikely. Lear himself was crushed to death thirty years before Czechoslovakia was born.

castigates the Mikado's cruelty; but this is not so: he thinks it is funny. Dickens and Bernard Shaw could be as funny as any other writer but they never laughed at the weak, the downtrodden, the sufferer. The Mikado mentions a torture which is 'something lingering, with boiling oil in it'; *H. M. S. Pinafore* contains many jolly references to the cat-o'-nine-tails; and even *The Gondoliers* – that feather-like, romantic tale – contains quite a few hints to the old nursemaid's memory being refreshed in the torture-chamber of the Inquisition. Gilbert's constant references to ageing women who ought to be thrown on the dust-heap are also numerous and well-known.

Evelyn Waugh also comes to mind. A great writer, a much less attractive human being. It is hard to decide whether one should find his cruelty or his snobbery more appalling – but we are discussing cruelty now. I could quote a number of examples from his novels but the one remark I most vividly recall comes from his Diaries. During the war, at the time of the London blitz he took his rare books down to the safety of his country house but sent his children up to the dangers of London. He thought that some people might think this decision strange, but explained that children were replaceable, rare books were not. (Which is not even true. Rare books are not unique, only rare, so they are replaceable; unique human beings are not.)

His son Auberon Waugh, while not replaceable, replaces his father to some extent. He is witty and often brilliant but – perhaps not surprisingly from a man whom his father valued less than his rare books – he is far too given to sneering and jeering. He often makes fun of old age, even of middle age, and of people who do not belong to the so-called upper classes – as if he himself were not hopelessly middle-class, and even more hopelessly middle-aged, with a balding head.

Voltaire was at least as witty as the whole Waugh

family put together and yet how much more noble and beautiful are *his* views on old age:

> On meurt deux fois, je le vois bien,
> Cesser d'aimer et d'être aimable
> C'est une mort insupportable,
> Cesser de vivre, ce n'est rien . . .*

I could continue my examples almost indefinitely but I shall stop here. I only meant to give a few examples. The question is this: if English humour has its nasty, cruel and repulsive elements, does that mean the English are nasty, cruel and repulsive people? Not at all.

First of all, joking about your phobias – death, old age, disease, torture – is usually not a sign of toughness and cruelty but of weakness and cowardice.

It is enough to spend a week or two in Britain to see that the British are not harsh and cruel people. Even if their virtues – as I have argued – are not what they used to be, cruelty is certainly not among their newly acquired vices. They are, as a nation, kind and courteous, helpful and considerate. In their colonial days they could be blindly selfish but they were rarely cruel. In any case the days of colonialism are over.

If all this is true, the problem becomes even more puzzling. Why do these gentle and kind people express themselves in a crueller type of humour than other, nastier and crueller societies? The explanation is simple. All peoples have to get rid of a certain amount of nastiness, frustration and hatred, just as a combustion engine must spit out its burnt and stinking waste. Some other people *commit* murderous and horrible acts; the British get rid

---

* In improvised translation:
We all die twice. (A thought that makes me queasy.)
To cease being loved or cease to love –
Save me from that, oh Heavens above!
But to cease to live? That's easy.

of their nastiness in the form of jokes about torturers, murderers, cannibalism and burning young ladies of Smyrna to death then they feel relaxed – also a little cleaner and relieved of tensions. They, too, have found their permissible outlet and can settle down to a life of leisure and to the luxury of decency.

# Political Jokes

TAKE TWO JOKES. One English.

A Tory canvasser called on an old farm labourer to ask for his vote.

'I vote Socialist,' said the old man, 'like my father and grandfather before me.'

'On that line of argument,' replied the canvasser derisively, 'what would you vote if your father was a fool and his father before him was a fool too?'

'In that case, I'd vote Conservative.'

And the other joke, coming from Nazi-occupied Norway in the days of the Second World War.

In a Norwegian village inn the local mayor, a well-known collaborator, was confronted by a patriot who asked him: 'What are you going to do when the Germans lose the war then?'

'Lose the war? Impossible!' snapped back the mayor. 'But if by any chance it should happen, then I'll just put my hat on and . . .'

'Put your hat on *what*?' inquired the patriot.*

Both these jokes still raise a smile or a laugh when told today in a pub or a drawing room in London or Oslo. Yet the difference between the two is enormous. A political joke in England, or in any other democracy, is simply

---

* These two jokes and one or two further down are quoted from the *Big Red Joke Book* by Greg Benton and Graham Loomes, Pluto Press, London, 1976.

a joke the subject of which happens to be politics. No one is in the slightest danger when telling it and the idea of danger just doesn't come into one's mind. Even Tories would laugh at the first one although, as likely as not, they would turn it into an anti-Socialist joke when retelling it. But in Nazi-occupied Norway the telling of the second joke might have resulted in being beaten to death or otherwise executed – as has, indeed, often happened to people who told jokes under Nazism, Fascism, Communism, and other forms of dictatorship, both right wing and left wing.

East German jokes on the subject make the situation clear: 'Is it true that Ulbricht collects political jokes?'

'No, he doesn't. He collects the people who tell them.'

Take a few more examples of jokes in various democracies, chosen from different periods. Here is one of the once-fashionable de Gaulle jokes.

The de Gaulles are waiting for the result of a plebiscite. The General is shaving and the first results are handed over by a messenger to his wife. Madame de Gaulle looks at the report, rushes into the bathroom and says to her husband: 'Mon Dieu, mon Dieu, we're winning!'

'I have already told you, Yvonne,' the General tells her coolly, 'that when no one else is present, you may call me Charles.'

Before the 1968 elections in America, there was only very limited enthusiasm for either candidate. People were fond of telling one another: 'Cheer up! Only one of them can be elected.'

When the Ayatollah Khomeini was establishing his new Islamic Republic with its horrible, retrograde laws, thieves' hands chopped off, adulterous women stoned to death, drinkers of alcohol flogged publicly, the story was told that the Shah sent a telegram to the Ayatollah: 'I hear you have established a peaceful regime in Iran. I wish to shake your hand. Please send it registered post.'

Many English politicians have heard jokes about themselves and had good laughs at them. I doubt that anyone dared tell a typical de Gaulle joke to de Gaulle but no one was afraid of the *political* consequence of telling such a joke. In America ten times more offensive jokes than the one quoted above are being told daily in clubs, bars and on television. The point is that in a democracy a political joke is just like any other joke.

Under tyrannies the political joke has an utterly different significance. Under oppressive regimes jokes replace the press, public debates, parliament and even private discussion but they are better than any of these. They are better because serious debate admits two sides, two views; a serious debate puts arguments which might be considered, turned round, rejected. As the tyrant does not allow his opponent the luxury of debate, it is only fair that he, too, should be deprived of the right of reply in some cases. The joke is a flash of lightning, a thrust with a rapier. It does not put forward the 'argument' that the tyrant may be mistaken; it makes a fool of him, pricks his pomposity, brings him down to a human level and proves that he is vulnerable and will one day come crashing down. Every joke told weakens the tyrant, every laugh at his expense is a nail in his coffin. That is why tyrants and their henchmen cannot possibly have a sense of humour. Rákosi – the bloodthirsty dictator of Hungary of the late forties and early fifties – tolerated no jokes against himself and many people paid with their lives for the jokes they had told; Kádár, perhaps not a paragon of Western-type democracy, but a milder, wiser and more humane man and no tyrant, insists that all anti-Kádár jokes should be brought to him.

No one living in the free atmosphere of Western democracy can imagine the liberating and invigorating effect these jokes have in a land of terror and intimidation as they are spread from mouth to mouth.

George Orwell wrote: 'Every joke is a tiny revolution. If you had to define humour in single phrase, you might define it as dignity sitting on a tin-tack. Whatever destroys dignity, and brings down the mighty from their seats, preferably with a bump, is funny. And the bigger the fall, the bigger the joke. It would be better to throw a custard pie at a bishop than at a curate. The truth is that you cannot be memorably funny without at some point raising topics which the rich, the powerful and the complacent would prefer to see left alone.'

George Orwell was a great writer and a clever man. But in spite of all his insight and all his hatred for Soviet tyranny and his joining the armies of Republican Spain, he remained an Englishman and even an old Etonian. He looked in the right direction and sensed the truth. But the 'destruction of dignity' and the raising of topics 'the rich, the powerful and the complacent' *would prefer to see left alone* is a far cry from the grim reality of Pastor Mueller sentenced to death by the Nazis for telling anti-Hitler jokes to an electrician who came to his house to repair a fuse.

The tyrant kicks back with desperation; the tellers of political jokes are persecuted, tortured and killed. The jokers often die; the jokes never. There was a story told in Stalin's Russia: a German, a Frenchman and a Russian meet and argue which nation is the bravest. The German and Frenchman make their respective claims and then the Russian says: 'No, the Russians are the bravest. They are sent to an arctic labour camp for telling jokes against Stalin, yet the jokes go on even in the camps.'

Three Soviet labour-camp inmates sat chatting one evening (says the *Big Red Joke Book*):

'What are you in for?' asked the first.

'Me? I spoke badly of Comrade Popov in 1939.'

'And you?'

'I spoke well of Comrade Popov in 1940. And what about you?' he asked turning to the third man.

'I am Comrade Popov.'

This joke, *mutatis mutandis*, was told in Louis Napoleon's France, Hitler's Germany, Stalin's Russia, the Colonels' Greece, Pinochet's Chile, Idi Amin's Uganda and, no doubt, will be told in many other countries for a long time. Jokes know no frontiers, they are always being renovated, rejuvenated, adapted to changing circumstances, and miraculously survive. 'Jokes about the German invasion of France in 1940,' say the authors, 'crop up again in Czechoslovakia in 1968. Jokes about anti-Semitism in Central and Eastern Europe at the turn of the century migrate across the Irish Sea to Ulster to cross the Atlantic to the United States, where they are used against white racism or Protestant ascendancy.'

Good jokes never die. (But some of them grow very, very old and feeble.)

The political joke is a short sharp shock against a given target. In Russia the mendacious press is often its victim.

Alexander the Great, Julius Caesar and Napoleon are watching the October Parade in Moscow's Red Square.

Alexander looks at the tanks and says: 'If I had chariots like these, I'd have conquered the whole of Asia.'

Caesar looks at the giant rockets: 'If I'd had such catapults, I'd have conquered the whole world.'

Napoleon looks up from a copy of *Pravda*: 'If I'd had a newspaper like this, nobody would ever have heard of Waterloo.'

In Russia, again, people are driven to despair by the constant promises of a rosy future and the dark and stark reality when that future becomes the present.

Two ex-members of the middle class meet in Moscow. One asks the other: 'Do you think we've already reached

'If I'd had a newspaper like this, nobody would ever have heard of Waterloo.'

one hundred per cent of Communism or will it get worse?'

Still in Russia, the terrible gap between glorious technology – SAM missiles and rockets sent up to Venus – and the miserably low standard of living is often emphasized.

'If things go on like this,' says a Soviet citizen, 'I'll soon have a helicopter.'

'A helicopter?' asks his friend. 'What do you need a helicopter for?'

'Of course I need it. Suppose we hear that you can buy shoe-laces in Smolensk. I fly to Smolensk and buy shoe-laces.'

In Eastern and Central Europe the Russians themselves have been the main targets of political jokes. The Russians were in many ways obviously inferior to the peoples they had subjugated, yet the latter had to sing Russia's praise and were ordered to try and emulate the great Russian achievements.

'What was the nationality of Adam and Eve?' people asked.

The answer: 'They were Russians. They went around naked, when they were hungry they had to steal apples, yet they were convinced that they were living in Paradise.'

There have been innumerable jokes explaining the differences between Capitalism and Communism. This one comes from Poland: 'Under capitalism there is rigid discipline in production and chaos in consumption. Under communism you get rigid discipline in consumption and chaos in production.'

Or again: 'What is the difference between Capitalism and Communism?'

'Capitalism is the exploitation of man by man. Communism is the other way round.'

Other jokes dealt with the horrible oppression of the Stalin years. It became known in Budapest that a mysterious three-fold coffin had been found at the bottom of the Danube. It had long been thought that Attila the Hun – a revered hero in Hungary – had been buried there and it had always been hoped that one day his coffin might be found.

'The man in the coffin,' a member of the Secret Police reported, 'is definitely Attila.'

'How do you know?'

'He confessed.'

Another line of jokes dealt with the so-called Russian generosity. All the satellite countries had incessantly to utter noises of deep gratitude while the Russians were ruthlessly exploiting them.

'Russian agriculture is so developed,' says a Russian, 'that they now have four harvests a year.'

'Aren't you exaggerating a bit?'

'No. One in the Soviet Union, one in Hungary, one in Poland, one in East Germany.'

On the same theme: there was a so-called Danubian Conference in Budapest, to decide navigation rights between Hungary and Russia. It was, of course, a fore-gone conclusion that Russia would give the orders and the Hungarians would obey, with gratitude. On the very first day of the Conference people in Budapest told one another: 'Agreement has already been reached. The Russians have the right to navigate the Danube length-wise and we across.'

Finally, East Germany was – and to some extent still is – a special case. Ulbricht was detested even more than other leaders were detested in neighbouring countries, particularly for his absolute subservience to the Soviet Union. Many East German jokes dealt with this subject. Two examples:

An old Russian comrade visits Ulbricht, goes to his study and sees a telephone on his desk with an earphone but no mouthpiece.

'What on earth is this?' he asks.

'This is my hot line to Moscow.'

Or another Ulbricht story: Khrushchev and Ulbricht are going around in Moscow. Khrushchev stops a small boy in the street and asks him: 'Who is your father?'

'Comrade Khrushchev.'

'Your mother?'

'The Soviet Union.'

'What would you like to be?'

'An astronaut.'

A few weeks later they meet again in East Berlin. This time it is Ulbricht who stops a small boy in the street.

'Who's your father?'

'Comrade Ulbricht.'

'Your mother?'

'The German Democratic Republic.'

'What would you like to be?'

'An orphan.'

# Dirty Jokes

'CONTINENTAL PEOPLE have sex life; the English have hot-water bottles.' This was the whole of the chapter on sex I wrote, soon after the war, in my book *How to be an Alien* and I shall never live it down. In subsequent years things seemed to have changed considerably and London was proclaimed (by Londoners) the sex capital of the world. I was unconvinced. When asked by a television interviewer (with a superior smile on his lips) whether I still believed that the English had nothing but hot-water bottles or did I think that they had progressed somewhat, I admitted that yes, they had progressed. Nowadays they had electric blankets.

People keep pointing out to me that the English multiply somehow and survive as a nation. That's true. Surprising but true.

The sex-life of the British, I have said in another book,* is in strange contradiction with their placid temperament. In everything else (e.g. queueing, driving) they are reserved, tolerant and disciplined; in their sex-life – if they live any sex-life at all – they tend to be violent and crude. A surprisingly large number of Englishmen like to be flogged by ladies wearing black stockings and nothing else; they believe that those ubiquitous places where women strip and show themselves naked to an audience for a modest fee, are evidence of virility; they

---

* *How to be Decadent*, André Deutsch, 1977.

think that the high circulation of porn magazines is a sign of high sexuality and not of high neurosis. They fail to see why sweating, topless waitresses should put you off food *and* sex at one and the same time.

The fact remains that England may be a copulating country but it is not an erotic country. Whenever I try to personify sex in England, Lord Longford and Mrs Whitehouse – these staunch guardians of our virtues – spring to mind. Girls are being taken to bed, to be sure, but they are not courted; they are being made love to but they are not pursued. Women are quite willing to go to bed but they rarely flirt with men. Ladies between the ages of eight and eighty (let's say eighty-five) come back from Italy outraged and complaining bitterly about the crude wolf-whistles. Crude they may be, but they do make middle-aged ladies feel twenty-five years younger, wanted and desired, and these complaints are just disguised boasts. When bishops, retired brigadiers or at least young executives start wolf-whistling in this town of ours, then I may believe that London has become – well, not the sex capital of the world but a budding sex-village.

So what is the position of sex jokes in English humour? Dirty jokes are common all over the world and most of the jokes told – eighty-five per cent of them, according to expert estimates – are sex jokes.

I personally detest jokes in general and dirty jokes in particular. I can enjoy a really good joke well told, particularly when it has an *à propos* and brings out a point or illuminates an argument. But when people blurt out one joke after the other for a whole evening, hour after hour, that makes me cry. 'Did you hear the latest?' they ask and then proceed to tell you jokes which had long white beards even under Victoria, Napoleon III, Francis Joseph or Abraham Lincoln (these jokes travel fast round the world). But my complaint is not really against the age of these jokes. Even the most brilliant of them becomes a trifle tedious when it is the 125th in a series. That is why I described my hobby in *Who's Who* as: not listening to funny stories. (The result is that people come up to me, saying: 'I know you don't like listening to jokes but just listen to this one' . . . and then they proceed to tell me one which used to be extremely popular in Wallenstein's army during the Thirty Years War. I sigh. I have recognized by now that this is a professional hazard. Most people define a humorist as the man *to whom* they must tell funny stories. While in this same parenthesis, I should like to make it clear that well-told personal anecdotes – things which actually happened to you or a friend of yours and which apply to a specific situation or tend to illustrate a point – belong to an utterly different category. Indeed, they are the spice of life. A few years ago, I spent an evening in Athens with a Greek writer and his charming and much younger wife. I had my equally charming and also much younger girl-friend with me. When he started telling a story, his wife exclaimed: 'For goodness' sake, Antony, not that one again!' When my turn came, my girl-friend interrupted: 'Please . . . please . . . I've heard that a hundred times!' So it went on, until Antony, very politely and calmly, turned to his wife and said: 'My dear, when a man's wife is bored with a man's stories, there is one thing he can do: change his wife. He cannot possibly change his stories.' Wise words. Personal anecdotes are the accumulated wealth of a life-time. A man cannot change his stories any more easily than he can change his nose or his left foot.)

Jokes on the not too temperamental sex-life of the English, in line with my own hot-water bottle jibe, are numerous.

A German businessman invites an Englishman for a round of golf.

'I don't play golf,' replies the Englishman. 'I tried it once and found it an excruciating bore so I gave it up.'

A little later the Englishman is offered a drink.

'I don't drink. I tried some whisky once and found the taste abominable. Never again, thank you.'

Then a young man comes into the room. The Englishman introduces him to his German friend: 'My son.'

The German looks at the boy and says: 'Your only child, I presume.'

Another joke in the same vein:

An English commercial traveller arrives at a village with no hotel, so he is put up in the house of the publican. The publican's wife has just made an apple pie which she leaves on the kitchen table when they all go to bed. As the house has only one bed, the publican sleeps between his wife and his guest. Fire breaks out during the night and the publican rushes down to deal with it. His wife whispers to the guest: 'This is your chance.'

Upon which the man jumps up, runs down to the kitchen and eats the apple pie.

And the last example.

A man goes out to an official dinner and rings up his wife some time later.

'I thought this was a business-function pure and proper. But there are a lot of girls here, some topless, the others quite naked, serving people and even sitting on our laps. What shall I do?'

His wife: 'If you think you can do anything, come home quickly.'

If all humour is aggressive, sex jokes are the most aggressive of the lot. Gershon Legman, an American, published an 811-page book on the dirty joke.* He regards the sexual joke as thinly disguised aggression. The very first sentence of the Introduction says: 'Under the mask

---

* *Rationale of the Dirty Joke*, Jonathan Cape, 1969.

of humour, our society allows infinite aggression by everyone against everyone.'

The person who has to listen to sex jokes is often a victim or butt. Compulsive story tellers force their jokes on victims, friends, and members of their own family. Yet, as I have already mentioned, these are the most popular type of jokes, particularly if the humour of scatology is thrown into the same category, as it should be. The teller of sex jokes, says Legman, feels fear or anxiety and by telling his jokes he wishes to expose the listener to the same fear and anxiety.

Freud put it differently in his *Wit and its Relation to the Unconscious*:

'The smutty joke is like a denudation of a person of the opposite sex toward whom the joke is directed. Through the utterance of obscene words, the person attacked is forced to picture the parts of the body in question, or the sexual act and shown that the aggressor himself pictures the same thing. There is no doubt that the original motive of the smutty joke was the pleasure of seeing the sexual displayed.'

As tellers of dirty jokes are mostly men and their so-called victims in most cases are women, Freudians regard sex jokes as verbal rape or, at least, preparation for physical approach.

Many of the jokes are degrading to women. The dirty joke, according to Freud, is a slightly more sophisticated form of other nasty habits: whispering dirty words to women in the street or writing up four-letter words – usually the name of the female genital organ – on walls.

Perhaps the significance and the character of all this has changed since Freud's time. Sex is not less important but it is not the dark and sinister secret it used to be. Most women are ready to acknowledge that they possess sexual organs and the majority would not dream of denying that they lead a normal sex-life, whether they are married or not. And indeed, quite a few charming and educated young ladies use obscene words which make *me* blush. The war between the sexes goes on, the struggle is eternal; sex can make people desperately unhappy today, just as it could a hundred, two hundred and two thousand years ago. But to speak of knickers, breasts and love-making today is quite definitely not half as aggressive as it used to be under Queen Victoria.

The few jokes quoted above are about the English; they are not English sex jokes. I have studied many books with so-called English sex jokes in them and found them disappointing. Foreign books – telling so-called English jokes – picture silly and old-fashioned stereotypes, the Englishmen in these stories are either stupid snobs or homosexuals or both; worse still, the jokes as jokes are, on the whole, rather feeble. A number of American jokes I came across were based on linguistic differences and were hardly more than puns.

According to Legman there *are* national characteristics in sex jokes. The Germans and the Dutch are especially addicted to scatology, 'doubtless a reaction', he explains, 'to excessively strict and early toilet-training'. I have often wondered why the mention of the posterior of the human body in Germany, or instructing someone to 'kiss my arse' in Austria, was regarded as a superb joke inspiring uproarious laughter. The behind is regarded as an extremely funny part of the body in America, too.

According to Renatus Hartog, a Dutchman, most French sex jokes deal with sexual technique and cuckolding.

Someone tells his neighbour: 'Listen, you forgot to pull the blinds last night and we were watching you making love to your wife.'

The man shakes his head merrily: 'The joke is on you. I wasn't even at home last night.'

This is, of course, a French joke; it could not be an English one.

So what is an English sex joke?

A few of them have real charm.

A girl of six asks another little girl of five: 'Are you a virgin?'

The little one blushes and replies: 'Not yet.'

The next one would be classified by psychologists as a penis-envy joke.

A little girl sees a little boy peeing and tells her mother: 'Mummy, I want one of those.'

Her mother replies: 'If you are a good girl you will get one later.'

Upon which her father butts in: 'And if you are a naughty girl, you'll get a lot of them.'

Jokes about the little innocent girl are very old. Today the little innocent girl is not quite as innocent as she used to be.

A little girl asks another: 'What are you doing in that old man's flat every afternoon?'

'Oh, I have to play with his penis and he gives me 20p.'

'Penis? what is a penis?'

'It's just like a cock, except it's soft.'

There are plenty of English jokes about male size – just as there are everywhere else in the world.

A little boy goes with his French nanny to the zoo and sees the elephant having an enormous erection.

'What's that?' asks the little boy.

The nanny is very embarrassed, and replies: 'Nothing.'

A cockney standing by remarks: 'Ain't she spoilt?'

Betting is a great passion of the English, and naturally enough betting and sex have been connected in many jokes.

A father visits his son's teacher and tells her that something must be done because the boy is on the way to becoming an obsessive gambler. He makes bets on everything all the time. The teacher promises to do what she can.

Next day the boy tells the teacher that she looks like someone who is having her period. The teacher tells the boy that he is wrong. Oh no, says the boy, he is quite sure, in fact he is ready to bet fifty pence. Very well, says the teacher, takes him into the common-room, locks the door, lifts her skirt, pulls her pants down and supplies the required proof. The boy pays her the fifty pence.

Next day the father appears again, even more worried.

'I hope,' says the teacher, 'that this taught him a lesson.'

'Like hell it did,' says the father. 'Yesterday morning he bet me five pounds that before evening he was going to see your pussy.'

Quite a few jokes, naturally, are connected with the declining economic situation. The following joke used to be told about various East European countries in the fifties, but it has reached Britain now and probably the United States as well. A man appears in a Paris brothel (never mind that there are no brothels in Paris; in jokes there are) and Madame delegates young Mimi for the task but she runs down the stairs after five minutes and is quite indignant: 'No. Not that. Certainly not.'

Madame sends up the more experienced Fifi, with the same result. She is fuming, too: 'No. Not that . . . out of the question.'

Madame frowns and goes up herself. But two minutes later she, too, comes down looking furious.

A man, an old habitué, gets curious and asks Madame, who is not put off too easily, 'What the hell does he want?'

'He wants to pay with Hungarian money.'

Britain being a very literate country, some of its dirty jokes have literary connotations.

A young man is sitting in a Rolls-Royce in darkest Mayfair, waiting for someone and smoking a cigar. A prowler goes by and knocks on the window of the car. The owner rolls the window down: 'What is it?'

'Look, Guv'nor, I am a bit hard up, d'you think you could lend me 20p for a cup of tea?'

The man in the Rolls replies: 'Neither a lender nor a borrower be. William Shakespeare' – and rolls his window up.

The prowler is taken aback and walks away. But he stops after a few steps, turns back and knocks again on the window. Down comes the window again.

'What is it now?'

'Cunt. D. H. Lawrence.'

And, finally, two jokes, which could not possibly be English. Their whole spirit, atmosphere and mentality are utterly alien to the British. The first is a Jewish joke (and more of them presently) which I heard in Hungary from a wonderful old prima donna, the idol of the nation.

Kohn and Gruen (the Central European heroes of many jokes) are playing cards and Gruen is losing heavily. He is very angry, and wants to needle Kohn, to make him lose concentration.

'I say, Kohn, you know that Schwartz is having an affair with your wife?'

No reaction. Kohn goes on playing.

'He calls on her every afternoon at two and takes her out.'

Kohn does not seem to hear, he plays on.

'It's half past two now. I would say it is just now that he climbs on her. This very moment.'

Kohn puts his cards down and asks: 'Listen, Gruen – are we playing cards seriously or are we gossiping?'

The other joke is also a Central European one. There is no racial problem there between black and white but many

*'A Romanian officer does not accept money.'*

of the nations and nationalities hate each other and love telling nasty and unfair jokes about people they dislike.

The butt of this pre-war joke is Romania.

A Romanian lieutenant goes to another Balkan country and accompanies home a famous courtesan. He spends the night with her and is about to leave in the morning. He is girding on his sword when the lady asks him: 'I say, what about money?'

He clicks his heels and salutes: 'A Romanian officer does not accept money.'

# Jewish Jokes

If the English can smile at themselves, the Jews can positively roar with laughter at their own weaknesses and peculiarities. A nation must have a great deal of self-confidence to be able to laugh at itself and both these peoples – the English and the Jews – know perfectly well, who are the most excellent and admirable people in the world . . . although their answers to this question are not identical.

Many people – I am one of them – think that Jewish jokes are the best of all. They are not only funny but are often wise and profound, revealing as much about human nature, the secrets of the human soul, as a good poem.

The Jewish sense of humour must be one of the decisive factors in the Jews' survival of thousands of years of persecution and diaspora. If you take your oppressors and persecutors seriously, you will sooner or later adopt their valuation of yourself; you will feel guilty and you will see yourself through their eyes. Take despots seriously and you will be broken by them and will, eventually, perish. But if you are able to laugh at them – see their stupidity, their vanity, their meanness – if you realize the fatuity of their claims to superiority, then oppression will steel you, make you stronger, more united as a group; and victory – or at least liberation – becomes possible. I am sure that the Jews of antiquity, wandering in the desert for forty years, were sustained not only by prayer, by Moses' strength of character and by manna from heaven, but also by primordial Jewish jokes.

But a lot of people have grave doubts about this thesis. Take this joke, for example, a product of Jewish humour in Czarist Russia.

An old Jew is travelling on a train. A young and smug officer is the only other passenger in the compartment. The officer does not like the idea of being closeted with the old Jew for a long journey so he is silent and aloof for a long time. But in the end he gets bored and starts talking to the other man who is having his lunch now, from a brown paper parcel, placed on his knees.

'I say, Jew,' says the lieutenant, 'you all have the reputation of being so clever.'

'Well, perhaps we are.'

'Are you? . . . Then tell me what makes you so clever?'

'Oh, I can tell you that easily,' says the old man. 'The heads of fish.'

'What d'you mean "the heads of fish"?' asks the officer, astonished.

'Yes . . . You see, the fish have wonderful brains. We eat them – and that's all.'

The officer is incredulous but the journey is long and one should try everything once, so he says: 'Very well. Will you sell me a couple of those fish-heads you have there?'

'With pleasure. It will be one rouble each.'

The officer buys two fish-heads and starts munching them with the greatest disgust. Suddenly he exclaims: 'I say, Jew . . . A whole herring costs only 50 kopeks. And you have sold me just the head of one for twice that price, a whole rouble.'

The Jew nods with satisfaction: 'You see . . . It's working already . . .'

This joke shows up the Russian officer as very stupid. But it also shows up the old Jew as a clever rogue who takes advantage of the lieutenant's stupidity. The joke reflects an ability to mock oneself, but it also seems to accept the anti-semitic image of Jews. It is a ghetto-joke, many people maintain; a Yiddish joke.

In Israel there is a great deal of hostility towards the Yiddish spirit and the Yiddish language. Some people revere it as an old tradition, but many young Israelis reject Yiddish as the culture of the ghetto. The ghetto may be the shame of the oppressors, not the shame of the Jews, but all the same, young Israelis do not cherish that phase of Jewish history. And this rebellious feeling, while it may be responsible for valuable gains, it is also responsible for a great loss.

The loss is this. Jewish humour got more or less lost in transit to Israel. Jewish jokes still reign supreme except in that country. The Jewish sense of humour – as I have said earlier – was an effective shield against ruthless, brutal oppression but the Jews of Israel are no longer oppressed. They are a new nation, burning with a new nationalism and the Jewish sense of humour is being replaced by the sense of humour of a new, developing nation, the sense of humour of Uganda or Upper Volta.

Other, more aggressive and sterner qualities are needed in Israel today than the mild self-mockery of the Polish-Jewish jokes. There is a new, precarious half-peace in that region but Israel was forced long ago to become a military camp, the Prussia of the Middle East.

The old spirit, however, if not exactly flourishing is not yet dead. I heard this story about the Six Day War.

A middle-aged man in his fifties goes to the Colonel on the first day of the war and volunteers his services. He is told that he is too old but he goes on pestering the Colonel who in the end tells him: 'Very well. Take these 5000 leaflets, go up to the Arab lines just in front of us, get rid of them and come back.'

The man returns six hours later and asks for another

job. The Colonel shakes his head: 'I've told you you are no good. What the hell were you doing for six hours?'

The man gets a little indignant! 'What was I doing, Colonel? Do you think it's all that easy to sell 5000 Jewish leaflets to those Arabs?'

This is, of course, the old-style Polish-Jewish joke about the cunning and slyness of the Jew who is slightly crooked but much cleverer than his adversary. It seems that the old-fashioned Jewish joke – miraculously – survives somehow even in Israel.

Things seem to have come to a full circle. I have told this story – not a joke, a true story – in another book but I have to repeat it here.

An Israeli couple are touring Europe with their eleven-year-old son. In Italy the boy asks his parents: 'Are these people Jews?'

'No, my boy,' his father tells him, 'they are Christians.'

In Germany he asks again: 'Are *these* people Jews?'

He is told in Germany, in Holland, and in Sweden: 'No, these people are not Jews, they are Christians.'

Finally he exclaims with genuine sympathy: 'Poor Christians! . . . It must be awful for them to be scattered like that all over the world.'

The butt of the Jewish joke is, more often than not, the Jew himself. About the Jewish hostess: 'Please, have another piece of cake, Herr Levy.'

'No, thank you. I have already had two.'

'You had four. But who's counting?'

The 'Jewish Mamma' jokes are innumerable. This one reflects her love and paranoia: a Mamma buys two shirts for her son's birthday. He – to please his mother – goes into the other room and puts one on immediately. When he comes back, she looks at him anxiously and asks: 'You don't like the other one?'

Religion, particularly the clever twisting of the Talmud, is another favourite subject.

A Jew in a small Polish village goes to the rabbi and tells him: 'Rabbi, I'm worried. The Talmud says that whenever you drop a piece of bread and butter, it always falls on the buttered side. Today I've dropped a piece and it fell on the non-buttered side.'

'Well,' says the rabbi, 'this was an exception.'

'No, no, Rabbi. There should be no exceptions . . . The Talmud says *always*.'

The rabbi scratches his head and tells the man to come back the next day, he will look it up. The man comes back and the rabbi tells him: 'Yes, the Talmud does say that the bread and butter *always* falls on the buttered side. And, of course, it always does. All that's happened was that you, stupid man, buttered the wrong side of the bread.'

Jews and the law is another vast subject. When I was a law student in Budapest, one of my professors illustrated many important theses with Jewish jokes. How right he was. These are the points I remember best even today. This story had to illustrate something of the responsibility of the man who accepts deposits.

Kohn and Gruen – the two permanent and immortal characters of these jokes – go to the rabbi and bring 10,000 crowns, a sizeable fortune, with them. They are planning some business together, they say, but they do not trust each other so will the rabbi keep that money. He is not to release it either to Kohn or to Gruen, only to the two together.

Three days later Gruen comes up and asks for the money. The rabbi shakes his head. 'You know perfectly well what the conditions are. You must come together.'

'But Rabbi,' says Gruen, 'Kohn knows all about it, he asked me to collect the money . . .'

The rabbi is adamant but Gruen goes on: 'Look out of the window, Rabbi. Kohn knows that I am here, he is standing down there at the corner, waiting for me.'

The rabbi looks out of the window, Kohn indeed is there, waiting.

Gruen goes on talking and in the end the rabbi gives in and hands the money over.

Next day Kohn comes to see him in despair. 'What did you do, Rabbi? . . . Gruen is a swindler, a thief . . . He got the money out of you and escaped to America. I shall never see him or my money again. I am ruined. I am awfully sorry, Rabbi, but I shall have to sue you for the money.'

And he does. At the trial the rabbi's defence is this:

'It is true that it was an absolute condition that I must not give the money to either of them, only to the two together. I have honoured that condition and intend to honour it in the future. It is true that I have given 10,000 crowns *from my own money* to Gruen but that has nothing to do with Kohn. If and when Kohn and Gruen come *together* to claim *their* 10,000 crowns they can have it.'

New York Jewish jokes have a special flavour.

A woman is travelling in a half-empty bus in Brooklyn. She asks the driver: 'Driver, are you Jewish?'

'No', is the curt reply.

Two stops later: 'Are you Jewish, Driver?'

'I have already told you, lady, that I am not Jewish.'

Another two stops further: 'You *are* Jewish, Driver, aren't you?'

The man breaks down: 'Of course, I am Jewish.'

The lady scrutinizes him more closely: 'You don't look Jewish.'

I cannot imagine a better and more concise description of the habit of claiming all prominent people – after all, the driver is *the* man of authority in a bus – but as soon as they want to belong, rejecting them.

English and Jewish humour possess the same element of self-mockery, the ability to laugh at themselves. But I thought understatement was not a conspicuously Jewish habit. I was put right about that in Israel. An Israeli was boasting about his country, about their achievements, blowing his own trumpet at full blast, and then said something about typical Jewish understatement.

'Wait a minute,' I interrupted. 'You've just spoken at great length about the Israelis being the greatest of all nations, intellectually, militarily, in every possible way. You said they had no rivals on earth and they were just superb.'

He nodded agreement: 'Yes. But still an understatement.'

# *Part Two: Practice*

ENGLISH HUMOUR might be defined as the sum total of all humorous writing in English. Some examples of that follow here. The selection I have made is, inevitably, subjective. This is simply a dish, designed to whet the appetite.

I have tried to include typically English pieces which could not have been written by, say, a Swede or a Bulgarian.

Most of the pieces are personal favourites. On the other hand I am not particularly enamoured of limericks, yet I felt I had to include them as a specially English type of humorous verse.

The following pieces are mostly verses. I have left out nearly all prose, from the very English Charles Dickens to the equally English Evelyn Waugh and Stephen Potter, simply because the temptation to include too much would have been irresistible and the publishers have urged me to keep this volume – if possible – under 12,500 pages.

# Nonsense

## Lear

NONSENSE POETRY is an English invention, made famous by Edward Lear. What is it? According to the Encyclopaedia Britannica: '*Nonsense verse*. Humorous or whimsical poetry that differs from other comic poetry in its resistance to any rational or allegorical interpretation.' This is a bad definition but excellent nonsense. Nonsense poetry, far from defying all allegorical interpretation, *is allegorical interpretation itself.*

Its meaning, its deeper significance may be defined in two ways. It may be seen as the ultimate literary rebellion against an orderly universe; shaking off the unbearable chains of everyday orderliness and logic; the anarchist's triumph over Nature and Sense. People (I used to be one of them) are fond of saying that the English are the most law-abiding people in the world. Football hooligans and flagellation perverts do pose a problem, but exceptions are held to confirm the rule. The English obviously need a few outlets and nonsense poetry is one of these. The English find it a great relief to stand the world on its head and make it look absurd.

But I am inclined towards the second explanation for nonsense poetry: its essence is that it is *poetry*. Put down something meaningless and irrational with intense and deadly seriousness, and people will nod knowingly, be impressed and even overawed. Edward Lear does it with humour, charm and wisdom, so people refuse to see the beauty, the deeper meaning and the allegory in what he writes. A lot of people are silly enough to think that if something is funny it cannot be serious. They fail to see that Lear is a serious and often a very sad poet. He describes the world as it *should* be; as it could be. He invents words because he needs them and people laugh at these words. I laugh at them, too, because they are funny. But they are lovely words and there is profundity in their form and shape and smell. *Runcible* is not a word one can find in a dictionary, but it definitely ought to exist and mean *something*. On the other hand, its meaning should not be too precise (well, no meaning of any word is too precise). If it did exist, if it did find its way into a dictionary, it would be tamed, circumscribed and put in chains. As an ordinary, run-of-the-mill word it would have a limited meaning. As it is, it has all the meaning you care to attach to it. Far from being meaningless, its meaning is infinite. Nonsense *is* infinite and that is why it means much more than sheer, vulgar, commonsense.

Edward Lear was born in 1812, a hundred years before me and in the same year as Charles Dickens and Robert Browning. He was the twentieth of twenty-one children, and his mother – who had had enough by the time he arrived – wanted nothing to do with him. He was brought up by his sister Ann who gave him all the care and affection she could; but no amount of sisterly affection can make up for the lack of a mother's love. On top of this he was an ugly man, with a ridiculously ugly nose which could be described as runcible. Or that's what he thought of it, at any rate. I have examined it on many photographs and found nothing either particularly ugly or particularly enchanting in it. It's a nose. Runcible

*94*

it is, I agree. He had extremely bad eyes and was an epileptic. But he was also a man of irresistible charm and of great talent. His speciality was the drawing of animals and landscapes and at the age of twenty he was engaged by the London Zoo to draw parrots. He saw and observed parrots all day long; he heard parrots; he smelt parrots; he lived with parrots; he dreamt of parrots; he was convinced that he would be turned into a parrot one day and he was quite content – indeed, delighted – with the prospect.

One day in 1832 he was drawing parrots, in the Zoo, just as he always did, when Lord Stanley, the son and heir of the twelfth Earl of Derby, saw him at work and, having been impressed, invited him to Knowsley Hall near Liverpool – a large, beautiful and ramshackle thirteenth century castle – to live there and draw the animals in their private zoo. Lear accepted the invitation.

His moving to Knowsley, where he spent four years, changed his life. At first he was treated like any other employee and had his meals with the stewards. He was a shy man and this arrangement suited him. But later the aged Earl of Derby (who originated that most famous of race meetings which carries his name) noticed that the younger members of the family were often late for meals and could hardly wait to be allowed to leave again. He wanted to know the reason for this. He was told that the children just loved Mr Lear, laughed at the stories and verses he improvised on the spot, enjoyed his company and could hardly bear to part with him even for the duration of a meal. Lord Derby decreed that if he was such excellent company, he should have his meals with the family – the table could do with some reinforcements. Lear joined the table, as ordered, and never looked back. From a lonely, shabby existence in a rented room in London he was lifted into a very different world.

But his fate was changed even more significantly. Those funny little verses he invented for the Stanley children became so popular that Lear published them in book form. The title of it was *A Book of Nonsense* and it appeared under the pseudonym of Derry Down Derry. Lear was afraid of ruining his reputation as a serious painter with these trifles. The book was a huge and immediate success with children and adults alike. People were intrigued to know who Derry Down Derry was and, soon enough, Lear informed the public that he was the author. People did not like this revelation. On one occasion he travelled by train to Guildford, when two ladies with two children got in. The children were reading the *Book of Nonsense* and an elderly gentleman, another fellow-traveller, remarked that the nation must be grateful to a great nobleman for composing such a charming book. He explained that the author of the book was the Earl of Derby himself. The ladies said that they thought the author was a certain Mr Edward Lear. The elderly gentleman shook his head and told the ladies, with a knowing smile, that Lord Derby's Christian name was Edward and *Lear* was simply an anagram of *Earl*. This was too much for Lear. He overcame his shyness and declared that he was Edward Lear and the author of the book. He produced a number of letters addressed to him and other documentary evidence. The man fell silent but did not believe him.

Lear's nonsense poetry is not nonsensical poetry but poetical nonsense. It catches the imagination and often the heart; it amuses, it charms and sometimes saddens the reader. You may read the *Akond of Swat* as delightful nonsense; you may read it as the mocking of tyranny; or even an improved kind of *Waiting for Godot*. (I cannot recall at the moment who it was who summed up *Godot* by saying: 'There is less in it than meets the eye'.)

Lear was a man who suffered deep depressions, in those

days called melancholy. Emery Kelen in his book* tells a joke which he says (and I agree) fits Lear perfectly.

There was a sad man who went to a doctor and complained about his melancholy. The doctor examined him, and told him: 'I can't find anything wrong with you but I have some advice. There is a circus in town; go there tonight. You'll see a clown who is so funny that you won't stop laughing for a week.'

'Doctor,' said the patient, 'I am the clown.'

## THE AKOND OF SWAT

*Edward Lear*

Who or why, or which, or what,
      Is the Akond of Swat?

Is he tall or short, or dark or fair?
Does he sit on a stool or a sofa or chair,
      or SQUAT,
      The Akond of Swat?

Is he wise or foolish, young or old?
Does he drink his soup and his coffee cold,
      or HOT,
      The Akond of Swat?

Does he sing or whistle, jabber or talk,
And when riding abroad does he gallop or walk,
      or TROT,
      The Akond of Swat?

Does he wear a turban, a fez, or a hat?
Does he sleep on a mattress, a bed, or a mat,

---

* Emery Kelen: *Mr Nonsense: A Life of Edward Lear*, Macdonald & Janes, 1973.

or a COT,
The Akond of Swat?

When he writes a copy in round-hand size,
Does he cross his T's and finish his I's
with a DOT,
The Akond of Swat?

Can he write a letter concisely clear
Without a speck or a smudge or smear
or BLOT,
The Akond of Swat?

Do his people like him extremely well?
Or do they, whenever they can, rebel,
or PLOT,
At the Akond of Swat?

If he catches them then, either old or young,
Does he have them chopped in pieces or hung,
or SHOT,
The Akond of Swat?

Do his people prig in the lanes or park?
Or even at times, when days are dark,
GAROTTE?
O the Akond of Swat!

Does he study the wants of his own dominion?
Or doesn't he care for public opinion
a JOT,
The Akond of Swat?

To amuse his mind do his people show him
Pictures, or any one's last new poem,
or WHAT,
For the Akond of Swat?

At night if he suddenly screams and wakes,
Do they bring him only a few small cakes,
      or a LOT,
        For the Akond of Swat?


Does he live on turnips, tea, or tripe?
Does he like his shawl to be marked with a stripe,
      or a DOT,
        The Akond of Swat?


Does he like to lie on his back in a boat
Like the lady who lived in that isle remote,
      SHALLOTT,
        The Akond of Swat?


Is he quiet, or always making a fuss?
Is his steward a Swiss or a Swede or a Russ,
      or a SCOT,
        The Akond of Swat?


Does he like to sit by the calm blue wave?
Or to sleep and snore in a dark green cave,
      or a GROTT,
        The Akond of Swat?


Does he drink small beer from a silver jug?
Or a bowl? or a glass? or a cup? or a mug?
      or a POT,
        The Akond of Swat?


Does he beat his wife with a gold-topped pipe,
When she lets the gooseberries grow too ripe,
      or ROT,
        The Akond of Swat?


Does he wear a white tie when he dines with friends,
And tie it neat in a bow with ends,

or a KNOT,
    The Akond of Swat?


Does he like new cream, and hate mince-pies?
When he looks at the sun does he wink his eyes,
    or NOT,
      The Akond of Swat?


Does he teach his subjects to roast and bake?
Does he sail about on an inland lake,
    in a YACHT,
      The Akond of Swat?


Someone, or nobody, knows, I wot,
Who or which or why or what
      Is the Akond of Swat!


## THE POBBLE WHO HAS NO TOES

*Edward Lear*

The Pobble who has no toes
  Had once as many as we;
When they said, 'Some day you may lose them all';
  He replied, 'Fish fiddle de-dee!'
And his Aunt Jobiska made him drink
Lavender water tinged with pink,
For she said, 'The World in general knows
There's nothing so good for a Pobble's toes!'

The Pobble who has no toes
  Swam across the Bristol Channel;
But before he set out he wrapped his nose
  In a piece of scarlet flannel.
For his Aunt Jobiska said, 'No harm
Can come to his toes if his nose is warm;

And it's perfectly known that a Pobble's toes
Are safe – provided he minds his nose.'

The Pobble swam fast and well,
   And when boats or ships came near him
He tinkledy-binkledy-winkled a bell,
   So that all the world could hear him.
And all the Sailors and Admirals cried,
When they saw him nearing the further side,
'He has gone to fish, for his Aunt Jobiska's
Runcible Cat with crimson whiskers!'

But before he touched the shore,
   The shore of the Bristol Channel,
A sea-green Porpoise carried away
   His wrapper of scarlet flannel.
And when he came to observe his feet,
Formerly garnished with toes so neat,
His face at once became forlorn
On perceiving that all his toes were gone!

And nobody ever knew
   From that dark day to the present,
Whoso had taken the Pobble's toes,
   In a manner so far from pleasant,
Whether the shrimps or crawfish grey,
Or crafty Mermaids stole them away –
Nobody knew; and nobody knows
How the Pobble was robbed of his twice five toes!

The Pobble who has no toes
   Was placed in a friendly Bark,
And they rowed him back, and carried him up
   To his Aunt Jobiska's park.
And she made him a feast at his earnest wish
Of eggs and buttercups fried with fish;
And she said, 'It's a fact the whole world knows,
That Pobbles are happier without their toes.'

I should like to say here that in choosing examples I was not trying to discover little-known masterpieces. These are pieces for beginners – but ones which I feel sure more advanced pupils will be pleased to meet again.

## Dodgson

If Edward Lear's life was adventurous, eventful and varied, the life of Charles Lutwidge Dodgson was dull and monotonous ... or so it outwardly seems. But could a man have written *Alice in Wonderland* and *Alice Through the Looking-Glass* if he had really been uninteresting and commonplace?

Dodgson's outward life story may be told in a few words. He was born in 1832 (the year Lear met Lord Stanley), the son of the Reverend Charles Dodgson. He spent four years at Rugby, matriculated at Christ Church, Oxford, in 1850, took a first class honours degree in mathematics at Christ Church and was appointed Lecturer in Mathematics there. He stayed in that job until he retired, at the age of forty-nine. In his spare time he became a brilliant photographer – according to some, one of the best in the nineteenth century. Under his own name he wrote such books as *The Formulae of Plane Trigonometry* and *An Elementary Treatise on Determinants*. He died at Guildford in 1898, at the age of sixty-six.

Some biographers maintain that the great event of his life was meeting Ellen Terry. She was eighteen and breathtakingly beautiful. He – it is believed – fell in love with her; some allege that he wanted to marry her. Well, it is all 'it is believed' and 'some allege' because he never talked of his feelings, certainly never proposed to Miss Terry and never wrote one single line about his feelings for her in his diary. He never married.

Most biographers agree, however, that another meeting

was even more important in his life. In 1856 he met Alice Liddell when she was not yet four. He told her lots of wonderful stories inventing them when they went for walks together. One day Alice said: 'Oh, Mr Dodgson, I wish you would write out Alice's adventures for me.'

He did, under the pseudonym of Lewis Carroll. 180,000 copies of *Alice in Wonderland* and *Alice Through the Looking-Glass* were sold in his lifetime. The books also gave many phrases to the English language and many immortal characters to English folklore, from the Mad Hatter through Humpty-Dumpty to Tweedledum and Tweedledee. Yet, icily and on innumerable occasions, he persisted in saying: 'Mr Dodgson neither claims nor acknowledges any connections with the books not published under his name.' He wanted to be remembered as the author of *An Elementary Treatise on Determinants*.

Alexander Woollcott (among others) pointed out the discrepancy between 'the man [who] wrote the most enchanting nonsense in the English language' and the 'puttering, fussy, fastidious, didactic old bachelor'. But Professor Peter Alexander, himself a logician, comments: '. . . the will to escape was joined with the ability to escape; an ability which depended on a detailed knowledge of, and an interest in, logic. Without Dodgson the pedantic logician, Carroll the artist would have been of considerably less importance; there was no discrepancy.'*

Of course, there is no discrepancy. If we could only see, we could always discern the one, whole man in such apparently contradictory characters.

Many attempts have been made to explain Dodgson on different levels. He was a homosexual, they say; he was in love with Alice and the other little girls under ten

* The last quotes come from Roger Lancelyn Green's *Lewis Carroll*, The Bodley Head, 1960.

whose company he sought so eagerly (although it has never been alleged that he behaved improperly to any one of them). At one stage he did indeed take to photographing little girls with no clothes on but, it seems, got frightened and gave it up. It has also been said that he was in love with Alice's governess and used the little girl as a cover-up.

One simple and plausible explanation of his pursuit of children lies in the fact that he suffered from a terrible stammer. That disability made him aloof, lonely and shy. He could trust his pen; he could never trust his tongue. Perhaps it was his stammer that drove him to children. He could relax in their company. They even loved listening to his voice.

He was *one* man, a compact and complicated human unit like most of us. The logician and the writer of nonsense tales complemented each other, on most occasions beautifully and charmingly. Roger Green reports how the child actress, Isa Bowman, begged him in a letter for 'millions of hugs and kisses'. Mathematician Dodgson and artist Carroll united their forces to give this reply:

> Millions must mean 2 millions at least . . . and I don't think you'll manage it more than 20 times a minute – [a sum follows]. I couldn't go on hugging and kissing more than 12 hours a day; and I wouldn't like to spend *Sundays* that way. So you see it would take 23 *weeks* of hard work. Really, my dear child, *I cannot spare the time.*

Viscount Simon – who knew Dodgson, he was Simon's tutor at Christ Church – also quotes a riddle, typical of both Dodgson and Lewis Carroll.*

---

* In Derek Hudson's *Lewis Carroll*, Constable, 1954.

A man wanted to go to the theatre, which would cost him 1s 6d, but he only had 1s. So he went into a Pawnbroker's shop and offered to pledge his shilling for a loan. The Pawnbroker satisfied himself that the shilling was genuine and lent him 9d on it.

The man then came out of the shop with 9d, and the Pawnbroker's ticket for 1s. Outside he met a friend to whom he offered to sell the Pawnbroker's ticket and the friend bought it from him for 9d. He now had 9d from the Pawnbroker and another 9d from the friend and so was able to go to the theatre.

'The question is,' said Lewis Carroll, 'who lost what?'

# YOU ARE OLD, FATHER WILLIAM

*Lewis Carroll*

'You are old, Father William,' the young man said,
  'And your hair has become very white;
And yet you incessantly stand on your head –
  Do you think, at your age, it is right?'

'In my youth,' Father William replied to his son,
  'I feared it might injure the brain;
But now that I'm perfectly sure I have none,
  Why, I do it again and again.'

'You are old,' said the youth, 'as I mentioned before,
  And have grown most uncommonly fat;
Yet you turned a back-somersault in at the door –
  Pray, what is the reason of that?'

'In my youth,' said the sage, as he shook his grey locks,
  'I kept all my limbs very supple
By the use of this ointment – one shilling the box –
  Allow me to sell you a couple?'

'You are old,' said the youth, 'and your jaws are too weak
    For anything tougher than suet;
Yet you finished the goose, with the bones and the beak –
    Pray how did you manage to do it?'

'In my youth,' said his father, 'I took to the law,
    And argued each case with my wife;
And the muscular strength, which it gave to my jaw,
    Has lasted the rest of my life.'

'You are old,' said the youth, 'one would hardly suppose
    That your eye was as steady as ever;
Yet you balanced an eel on the end of your nose –
    What made you so awfully clever?'

'I have answered three questions, and that is enough,'
    Said his father; 'don't give yourself airs!
Do you think I can listen all day to such stuff?
    Be off, or I'll kick you downstairs!'


# THE WALRUS AND THE CARPENTER

*Lewis Carroll*

The sun was shining on the sea,
    Shining with all his might:
He did his very best to make
    The billows smooth and bright –
And this was odd, because it was
    The middle of the night.

The moon was shining sulkily
    Because she thought the sun
Had got no business to be there
    After the day was done –

'It's very rude of him,' she said,
  'To come and spoil the fun!'

The sea was wet as wet could be,
  The sands were dry as dry.
You could not see a cloud, because
  No cloud was in the sky:
No birds were flying overhead –
  There were no birds to fly.

The Walrus and the Carpenter
  Were walking close at hand;
They wept like anything to see
  Such quantities of sand:
'If this were only cleared away,'
  They said, 'it *would* be grand!'

'If seven maids with seven mops
  Swept it for half a year,
Do you suppose,' the Walrus said,
  'That they could get it clear?'
'I doubt it,' said the Carpenter,
  And shed a bitter tear.

'O Oysters, come and walk with us!'
  The Walrus did beseech.
'A pleasant walk, a pleasant talk,
  Along the briny beach:
We cannot do with more than four,
  To give a hand to each.'

The eldest Oyster looked at him,
  But never a word he said:
The eldest Oyster winked his eye,
  And shook his heavy head –
Meaning to say he did not choose
  To leave the oyster-bed.

But four young Oysters hurried up,
   All eager for the treat:
Their coats were brushed, their faces washed,
   Their shoes were clean and neat –
And this was odd, because, you know,
   They hadn't any feet.

Four other Oysters followed them,
   And yet another four;
And thick and fast they came at last,
   And more, and more, and more –
All hopping through the frothy waves,
   And scrambling to the shore.

The Walrus and the Carpenter
   Walked on a mile or so,
And then they rested on a rock
   Conveniently low:
And all the little Oysters stood
   And waited in a row.

'The time has come,' the Walrus said,
   'To talk of many things:
Of shoes – and ships – and sealing-wax –
   Of cabbages – and kings –
And why the sea is boiling hot –
   And whether pigs have wings.'

'But wait a bit,' the Oysters cried,
   'Before we have our chat;
For some of us are out of breath,
   And all of us are fat!'
'No hurry!' said the Carpenter.
   They thanked him much for that.

'A loaf of bread,' the Walrus said,
   'Is what we chiefly need:
Pepper and vinegar besides

Are very good indeed –
Now if you're ready, Oysters dear,
    We can begin to feed.'


'But not on us!' the Oysters cried,
    Turning a little blue.
'After such kindness, that would be
    A dismal thing to do!'
'The night is fine,' the Walrus said.
    'Do you admire the view?


'It was so kind of you to come!
    And you are very nice!'
The Carpenter said nothing but
    'Cut us another slice:
I wish you were not quite so deaf –
    I've had to ask you twice!'


'It seems a shame,' the Walrus said,
    'To play them such a trick,
After we've brought them out so far,
    And made them trot so quick!'
The Carpenter said nothing but
    'The butter's spread too thick!'


'I weep for you,' the Walrus said:
    'I deeply sympathize.'
With sobs and tears he sorted out
    Those of the largest size,
Holding his pocket-handkerchief
    Before his streaming eyes.


'O Oysters,' said the Carpenter,
    'You've had a pleasant run!
Shall we be trotting home again?'
    But answer came there none –
And this was scarcely odd, because
    They'd eaten every one.

*Gilbert*

I had spent only about six weeks in London when Dr Kiss, the Economic Editor of my Budapest newspaper, came over for a visit. That was – I have said it before – in 1938 and I, the paper's London correspondent, had to accompany such a senior member whenever I could. That was no great sacrifice as Dr Kiss was a charming and very erudite man. He knew English much better than I did, he had translated many English authors into Hungarian and I remember reading quite a few books by H. G. Wells in his translation. We were walking across Leicester Square when he saw a neon sign and exclaimed: '*The Mikado*! Let's go in!' My heart sank. 'But that's a musical,' I pleaded. 'An operetta.' 'Yes, it is,' he agreed. 'But there are operettas and operettas.'

In we went at three o'clock in the afternoon. For the first and last time in my life I sat through four performances of a film. If they had given four more performances, I would have stayed. Dr Kiss left after one performance, I had to be thrown out at eleven o'clock. I was enchanted and excited: this was a new, grotesque, yet – for me – perfectly sensible and impressive world. I enjoyed not only the wit but also the technical perfection of the verses; even the music made me laugh aloud with delight.

But as my English was far from perfect, I missed a lot. First thing next morning, I trotted over to the Times Book Club – the leading lending library of those days – and asked, rather timidly, whether *The Mikado* existed in print. I hardly expected to be able to obtain the libretto of a sixty-years-old operetta in book-form, but I got it. I had not read Keats, Shelley, Browning or Eliot in the original yet, but in a few weeks' time I knew all the verses of *The Mikado* by heart. And a few weeks later *Patience*, *The Pirates of Penzance*, *Iolanthe*, *Pinafore*, and *The Gondoliers* followed. I knew the main songs of these operas by heart long before I ever saw them on the stage. It was a long time before I learnt that Gilbert and Sullivan were not just a writer and a composer, but a cult – a national secret like cricket. I cannot, naturally, claim to be the greatest living Gilbert and Sullivan expert; but I am sure I am the greatest living Hungarian expert on them.

William Schwenck Gilbert was born in London, near the Strand, on November 18, 1836. He is a real Victorian in that Queen Victoria ascended the throne seven months after his birth. He got his middle name from some distant German relation and he detested it. During the Franco-Prussian war he was nearly arrested because of it, as the Parisians thought he was a Prussian spy. Gilbert's father, also called William, was a naval surgeon but when, at an early age, he inherited some money, he retired and wrote a few novels. Gilbert jr. first became a government clerk and stuck to the hated job for four years. But inheriting money is a favourite English folk-custom: it's constantly being done, often from long-forgotten aunts or cousins thrice removed. Gilbert was no exception: he inherited a few hundred pounds and later he said that it was the happiest day of his life when he was able to send his letter of resignation to the department of education. He entered himself as a student at the Middle Temple and read for the law. He was called to the bar and became an extremely unsuccessful barrister. In four years he had fewer than twenty briefs and made less than £100. But he loved the law; it formed his way of thinking and when he wrote that 'The law is the true embodiment of everything that's excellent' he really meant it.

While at the bar, he wrote innumerable plays, sketches, verses, libretti – all unperformed and unpublished. Everything was sent to theatres and editors; everything was rejected. In 1861 a new magazine, *Fun*, accepted one piece by him and the editor was so much impressed by his wit that he sent for him. Gilbert became a regular contributor to *Fun*, and later its dramatic critic. He wrote nearly all the *Bab Ballads* for *Fun*. He thought little of his comic verse and still less of his own drawings illustrating them. They were written – he said later – in a hurry, mostly because they were needed to fill in space. When they were published in book form he wrote – with quite uncharacteristic modesty – that he 'ventured to publish the little pictures with them, because while they are certainly quite as bad as the ballads, they are not much worse'.

The Ballads as well as the pictures are classics of English humorous literature. 'Though essentially English,' writes Hesketh Pearson,* 'nothing quite like them has been produced by any other Englishman. They contain both satire and nonsense, but these ingredients are merely incidental to their composition. They are simply jokes, and some people thought jokes in bad taste. But the quality that makes them unique and may make them immortal is the sudden imaginative perception that human beings and the condition of their existence on this planet are inherently ridiculous. While the imperfection of life is a source of sadness in the great poets, it is a source of silliness in "Bab", who created an art of utter absurdity.'

Underestimating his own achievements was not one of Gilbert's outstanding characteristics. He could not tolerate adverse criticism. (The favourable variety he tolerated with great patience, like the rest of us.) He was oversensitive, irascible, overbearing; but he was also honest and straightforward. He always meant what he said, and – worse – he always said what he meant. This was the real reason for his quarrel with Sullivan.

W. S. Gilbert and Arthur Sullivan had met fleetingly

---

* Hesketh Pearson: *Gilbert, His Life and Strife*, Methuen, 1957.

before the beginning of the Gilbert-and-Sullivan era proper. Indeed, they had written a little burlesque opera together for German Reed. It was called *Thespis* and it was a flop. The critic for *The Times* found Gilbert's story lively and original and Sullivan's music pretty and fascinating, so he was 'rather disappointed' that the public failed to respond to the piece. But that is what happened. *Thespis* was never revived.

Four years later, in 1875 the impresario Richard D'Oyly Carte, manager of the Royalty Theatre, was putting on a musical which was expected to be a great hit but which was short. Rather bravely, considering the dismal failure of *Thespis*, he asked Gilbert and Sullivan to collaborate on a little something to fill in time. The 'great hit' was a failure; the 'little something' is still being played today. It was *Trial by Jury*. Its first run lasted a year and Sullivan's brother Fred played the Learned Judge.

This one-act opera was followed by many other collaborations, among them *HMS Pinafore*, *The Pirates of Penzance*, *Patience*, *Iolanthe*, *The Mikado*, *The Yeomen of the Guard* and *The Gondoliers* – all sacred names for Gilbert and Sullivan addicts. The two men became rich and famous, but they could not stand each other. About fifteen years after *Trial by Jury* they quarrelled over the price of a carpet bought by D'Oyly Carte for the Savoy Theatre (which had been built to house their work, the 'Savoy Operas') and the partnership broke up. But that notorious quarrel about the carpet was not about the carpet at all. It was bound to erupt, carpet or no carpet, because of the clash of personalities. The two men complemented each other in many ways, but their differences were too great for the collaboration to endure: Gilbert's impulsive bluntness and touchiness and Sullivan's accommodating suavity, his hatred of disagreements and his eagerness to be loved by everyone, all the time, just would not mix.

Gilbert died by drowning in his own swimming-pool, in 1911. A young woman had got into trouble in the water and he rescued her, losing his own life in the process: an act not surprising in one who could be genuinely kind and generous. But basically he was a tough and cruel man, the typical mimophant. The mimophant – a zoological wonder invented by Arthur Koestler – is a cross between the mimosa and the elephant. The mimophant is touchy like the mimosa when he is concerned; but he is as lightfooted as an elephant when it comes to others. When Gilbert was being cross-examined by Carson in a silly libel-suit he initiated (and did not win), he was asked:

*Carson:* 'You don't like reading hostile criticism?'

*Gilbert:* 'I have a horror of reading criticism at all, either good or bad. I know how good I am, but I don't know how bad I am.'

During the same cross-examination Gilbert referred to bad musical comedies.

*Carson:* 'Give me the name of one.'

*Gilbert:* 'There are fifty of them.'

*Carson:* 'Give me one.'

*Gilbert:* 'I would say such a piece as the *Circus Girl*.'

*Carson:* 'Would you call it a bad musical comedy?'

*Gilbert:* 'I would call it bad. I believe the manager calls it a musical comedy.'

As Dickens lit up the early Victorian days, so did Gilbert and Sullivan sparkle, dazzle and delight life a few decades later.

I said about Lewis Carroll, that no writer, no person, can be two persons. What appears to be a dual personality always proves to be a complete and reasonable unit as soon as we get the clue to it. But if a person cannot be two persons, he can be half a person – at least in literature. Gilbert and Sullivan were two halves. With the exception of the *Bab Ballads* – charming, witty and original – one was not much without the other. Gilbert did write some successful plays, good plays, funny plays, worthy plays, but they would have been forgotten long ago but for his collaboration with Sullivan. And this is even truer for Sullivan. Sullivan was regarded as the great musician of his age, an English Haydn, or even more, and was often castigated for wasting his precious time on such trifles as the Savoy operas. He should be writing grand operas, oratorios and other immortal stuff. Well, he did – and if the grand stuff is remembered and performed at all, it is because he also wrote *The Gondoliers* and *The Yeomen of the Guard*, with Gilbert. After their quarrel they tried to prove that neither needed the other, but they failed to click with other partners. I know it will displease many of their admirers but I repeat: Gilbert is nothing without Sullivan, Sullivan is nothing without Gilbert. *Ivanhoe*, the grand opera, would have been thrown on the dustheap of musical history, if it were not for *The Mikado*. The flowers that bloom in the spring, tra-la, have a lot to do with the case.

## ETIQUETTE

*W. S. Gilbert*

The *Ballyshannon* foundered off the coast of Cariboo,
And down in fathoms many went the captain and the crew;
Down went the owners – greedy men whom hope of gain
    allured:
Oh, dry the starting tear, for they were heavily insured.

Besides the captain and the mate, the owners and the crew,
The passengers were also drowned excepting only two:
Young PETER GRAY, who tasted teas for BAKER, CROOP,
    AND CO,
And SOMERS, who from Eastern shores imported indigo.

These passengers, by reason of their clinging to a mast,
Upon a desert island were eventually cast.
They hunted for their meals, as ALEXANDER SELKIRK used,
But they couldn't chat together – they had not been
    introduced.

For PETER GRAY, and SOMERS too though certainly in trade,
Were properly particular about the friends they made;
And somehow thus they settled it without a word of mouth –
That GRAY should take the northern half, while SOMERS took
    the south.

On PETER'S portion oysters grew – a delicacy rare,
But oysters were a delicacy PETER couldn't bear.
On SOMERS' side was turtle, on the shingle lying thick,
Which SOMERS couldn't eat, because it always made him sick.

GRAY gnashed his teeth with envy as he saw a mighty store
Of turtle unmolested on his fellow-creature's shore:
The oysters at his feet aside impatiently he shoved,
For turtle and his mother were the only things he loved.

And SOMERS sighed in sorrow as he settled in the south,
For the thought of PETER'S oysters brought the water to his
    mouth.
He longed to lay him down upon the shelly bed, and stuff:
He had often eaten oysters, but had never had enough.

How they wished an introduction to each other they had had
When on board the *Ballyshannon*! And it drove them
    nearly mad
To think how very friendly with each other they might get,
If it wasn't for the arbitrary rule of etiquette!

One day, when out a-hunting for the *mus ridiculus*,
GRAY overheard his fellow-man soliloquising thus:
'I wonder how the playmates of my youth are getting on,
M'CONNELL, S. B. WALTERS, PADDY BYLES, and ROBINSON?'

These simple words made PETER as delighted as could be,
Old chummies at the Charterhouse were ROBINSON and he!
He walked straight up to SOMERS, then he turned
    extremely red,
Hesitated, hummed and hawed a bit, then cleared his throat,
    and said:

'I beg your pardon – pray forgive me if I seem too bold,
But you have breathed a name I knew familiarly of old.
You spoke aloud of ROBINSON – I happened to be by –
You know him?' 'Yes, extremely well.' 'Allow me – so do I!'

It was enough: they felt they could more sociably get on,
For (ah, the magic of the fact!) they each knew ROBINSON!
And MR SOMERS' turtle was at PETER'S service quite,
And MR SOMERS punished PETER'S oyster-beds all night.

They soon became like brothers from community of wrongs:
They wrote each other little odes and sang each other songs;
They told each other anecdotes disparaging their wives;
On several occasions, too, they saved each other's lives.

They felt quite melancholy when they parted for the night,
And got up in the morning soon as ever it was light;
Each other's pleasant company they reckoned so upon,
And all because it happened that they both knew ROBINSON!

They lived for many years on that inhospitable shore,
And day by day they learned to love each other more and
    more.
At last, to their astonishment, on getting up one day,
They saw a vessel anchored in the offing of the bay!

To PETER an idea occurred. 'Suppose we cross the main?
So good an opportunity may not occur again.'
And SOMERS thought a minute, then ejaculated, 'Done!
I wonder how my business in the City's getting on?'

'But stay,' said MR PETER: 'when in England, as you know,
I earned a living tasting teas for BAKER, CROOP, AND CO.,
I may be superseded – my employers think me dead!'
'Then come with me,' said SOMERS, 'and taste indigo instead.'

But all their plans were scattered in a moment when they
  found
The vessel was a convict ship from Portland, outward
  bound!
When a boat came off to fetch them, though they felt it very
  kind,
To go on board they firmly but respectfully declined.

As both the happy settlers roared with laughter at the joke,
They recognized an unattractive fellow pulling stroke:
'Twas ROBINSON – a convict, in an unbecoming frock!
Condemned to seven years for misappropriating stock!!!

They laughed no more, for SOMERS thought he had been
  rather rash
In knowing one whose friend had misappropriated cash;
And PETER thought a foolish tack he must have gone upon
In making the acquaintance of a friend of ROBINSON.

At first they didn't quarrel very openly, I've heard;
They nodded when they met, and now and then exchanged a
  word:
The word grew rare, and rarer still the nodding of the head,
And when they meet each other now, they cut each other
dead.

To allocate the island they agreed by word of mouth,
And PETER takes the north again, and SOMERS takes the
  south;
And PETER has the oysters, which he loathes with horror
  grim,
And SOMERS has the turtle – turtle disagrees with him.

## THE PLAYED-OUT HUMORIST

*W. S. Gilbert*

QUIXOTIC is his enterprise, and hopeless his adventure is,
  Who seeks for jocularities that haven't yet been said.
The world has joked incessantly for over fifty centuries,
  And every joke that's possible has long ago been made.
I started as a humorist with lots of mental fizziness,
  But humour is a drug which it's the fashion to abuse;
For my stock-in-trade, my fixtures, and the goodwill of the
      business
  No reasonable offer I am likely to refuse.
        And if anybody choose
        He may circulate The news
  That no reasonable offer I'm likely to refuse.


Oh happy was that humorist – the first that made a pun
      at all –
  Who when a joke occurred to him, however poor and
      mean,
Was absolutely certain that it never had been done at all –
  How popular at dinners must that humorist have been!
  Oh the days when some stepfather for the query held a
      handle out.
  The door-mat from the scraper, is it distant very far?
And when no one knew where Moses was when Aaron
      blew the candle out,
  And no one had discovered that a door could be a-jar!
        But your modern hearers are
        In their tastes particular,
  And they sneer if you inform them that a door can be
      a-jar!


In search of quip and quiddity, I've sat all day, alone, apart –
  And all that I could hit on as a problem was – to find
Analogy between a scrag of mutton and a Bony-part,
  Which offers slight employment to the speculative mind:

For you cannot call it very good, however great your charity –
　　It's not the sort of humour that is greeted with a shout –
And I've come to the conclusion that my mine of jocularity,
　　In present Anno Domini, is worked completely out!
　　　　　　Though the notion you may scout,
　　　　　　　I can prove beyond a doubt
　　That my mine of jocularity is utterly worked out!


# GENTLE ALICE BROWN

*W. S. Gilbert*

It was a robber's daughter, and her name was Alice Brown,
Her father was the terror of a small Italian town;
Her mother was a foolish, weak, but amiable old thing;
But it isn't of her parents that I'm going for to sing.

As Alice was a-sitting at her window-sill one day
A beautiful young gentleman he chanced to pass that way;
She cast her eyes upon him, and he looked so good and true,
That she thought, 'I could be happy with a gentleman
　　like you!'

And every morning passed her house that cream of
　　gentlemen,
She knew she might expect him at a quarter unto ten,
A sorter in the Custom-house, it was his daily road
(The Custom-house was fifteen minutes' walk from her abode).

But Alice was a pious girl, who knew it wasn't wise
To look at strange young sorters with expressive purple eyes;
So she sought the village priest to whom her family confessed –
The priest by whom their little sins were carefully assessed.

'Oh holy father,' Alice said, ''twould grieve you, would it not?
To discover that I was a most disreputable lot!

Of all unhappy sinners I'm the most unhappy one!'
The padre said, 'Whatever have you been and gone and
    done?'

'I have helped mamma to steal a little kiddy from its dad.
I've assisted dear papa in cutting up a little lad.
I've planned a little burglary and forged a little cheque,
And slain a little baby for the coral on its neck!'

The worthy pastor heaved a sigh, and dropped a silent tear –
And said, 'You mustn't judge yourself too heavily, my dear –
It's wrong to murder babies, little corals for to fleece;
But sins like these one expiates at half-a-crown apiece.

'Girls will be girls – you're very young, and flighty in your
    mind;
Old heads upon young shoulders we must not expect to find:
We mustn't be too hard upon these little girlish tricks –
Let's see – five crimes at half-a-crown – exactly
    twelve-and-six.'

'Oh, father,' little ALICE cried, 'your kindness makes me
    weep,
You do these little things for me so singularly cheap –
Your thoughtful liberality I never can forget;
But oh, there is another crime I haven't mentioned yet!

'A pleasant-looking gentleman, with pretty purple eyes, –
I've noticed at my window, as I've sat a-catching flies;
He passes by it every day as certain as can be –
I blush to say I've winked at him, and he has winked at me!'

'For shame,' said FATHER PAUL, 'my erring daughter!
    On my word
This is the most distressing news that I have ever heard.
Why, naughty girl, your excellent papa has pledged
    your hand
To a promising young robber, the lieutenant of his band!

'This dreadful piece of news will pain your worthy parents so!
They are the most remunerative customers I know;
For many many years they've kept starvation from my doors,
I never knew so criminal a family as yours!

'The common country folk in this insipid neighbourhood
Have nothing to confess, they're so ridiculously good;
And if you marry any one respectable at all,
Why, you'll reform, and what will then become of FATHER
    PAUL?'

The worthy priest, he up and drew his cowl upon his crown,
And started off in haste to tell the news to ROBBER BROWN;
To tell him how his daughter, who was now for marriage fit,
Had winked upon a sorter, who reciprocated it.

Good ROBBER BROWN he muffled up his anger pretty well,
He said, 'I have a notion, and that notion I will tell;
I will nab this gay young sorter, terrify him into fits,
And get my gentle wife to chop him into little bits.

'I've studied human nature, and I know a thing or two;
Though a girl may fondly love a living gent, as many do,
A feeling of disgust upon her senses there will fall
When she looks upon his body chopped particularly small.'

He traced that gallant sorter to a still suburban square;
He watched his opportunity and seized him unaware;
He took a life-preserver and he hit him on the head,
And MRS BROWN dissected him before she went to bed.

And pretty little ALICE grew more settled in her mind,
She never more was guilty of a weakness of the kind,
Until at length good ROBBER BROWN bestowed her
    pretty hand
On the promising young robber, the lieutenant of his band.

# Limericks and Clerihews

I AM NOT in love with the limerick, although I believe my reservations have more to do with the many tasteless and witless limericks in circulation than with any inborn limitation of the form itself. The limerick is regarded as a very English comic verse form although – according to some – its origin is French. This 'according to some' must be emphasized, because no one really knows anything definite about the origin of the limerick and no one really knows why it is named after a western Irish town or county.

Langford Reed devoted a great deal of energy to the study of limericks and he suggests: 'This peculiar form of verse was brought direct to Limerick by the returned veterans of the Irish Brigade, who were attached to the French army for a period of nearly a hundred years from 1691. The Brigade was based in Limerick and probably brought home a large number of barrack-room songs.' Others maintain that limericks are much older than that, originating in the fourteenth century.

More recently Mr G. Legman – whom we met in the chapter on sex jokes – has devoted two columns to the limerick. Mr Legman is interested only and exclusively in dirty limericks. This, he says, reflects no personal preference, only scientific requirements. (It was the same with the dirty joke.) He seems to be annoyed that people venture to write clean limericks at all. 'The clean sort of limerick,' he writes,\* 'is an obvious palliation, its content insipid, its rhyming artificially ingenious, its whole pervaded with a frustrated nonsense that vents itself typically in explosive and aggressive violence.' Why a man's rhyming should improve if he writes dirty limericks instead of clean ones is not explained. Mr Legman admits that aggressive bawdy limericks exist but he grows positively angry when he speaks of the 'silly delectation of a few elderly gentlemen, such as the late Langford Reed' whose great sin seems to have been to like clean limericks. He also quotes another American, Don Marquis, who said that there are three kinds of limericks: 'Limericks to be told when ladies are present; limericks to be told when ladies are absent but clergymen are present; and LIMERICKS.'

Mr Legman also says that limericks, in spite of their overwhelming dirt, are the folklore of the educated classes. 'Limericks are not liked by, nor consciously to be collected among working men, farm-hands, cowboys, sailors and other classic oral sources.'

Limericks do in fact, as Marquis said, fall more or less into classes. The first is the class of the dirty limerick. It is, as a rule, very dirty indeed, and rarely witty or even funny. I see no necessity for using many four-letter words in an ordinary book or article, meant for the general reader, but I use them sometimes when bowdlerization would look silly. Mr Legman's first volume contains 1952 limericks. I have read hundreds which I would willingly recite to ladies but certainly not to clergymen. But I feel I have to give a few examples, however reluctantly. I have chosen the relatively clean and relatively funny ones:

---

\* G. Legman: *The Limerick*, Volume I, Panther Books, 1976.

> There was a young lady from Spain,
> Who was fucked by a monk in a drain.
> They did it again,
> And again and again,
> And again and again and again.

(The admirable potency of the monk reminds me of a joke I recently heard in Hungary. An elderly gentleman asks another: 'Do you go out to pee between two love-makings?' – 'Always,' he replies. 'How could I withhold it for a month?')

I quote the next two from memory:

> An Argentine gaucho called Bruno
> Said: 'I know everything you know.
> A girl is fine,
> A boy is divine,
> But a llama is Numero Uno.'

Or one which is not really dirty, just naughty:

> There was a young girl from Cape Cod,
> Who thought babies were coming from God.
> But it wasn't Almighty
> Who lifted her nighty:
> It was Roger, the lodger, the sod.

The great fashion for limericks was initiated by Edward Lear. His *Book of Nonsense* contains many but I feel they are not among his best creations. The main trouble is that Lear's fifth line is usually a repetition (occasionally with slight variation) of the first and rarely adds anything to the joke. More often it is a point which does not come off. Lear's nonsense poetry is often meaningful and even profound, his limericks are more often than not just plain silly, no more than a grotesque literary grimace. There is nothing wrong, of course, with silliness or with literary grimaces but they belong to a different category from, say, the *Owl and the Pussycat*.

There was an old person of Annerly
Whose conduct was strange and unmannerly.
He rushed down the strand
With a pig in each hand
But returned in the evening to Annerly.

The last line here varies more than usual. So the example is not really an example. Or rather it is a typical example of examples: it does not prove the point. A more typical one:

There was an Old Man with a nose,
Who said, 'If you choose to suppose,
  That my nose is too long,
  You are certainly wrong!'
That remarkable Man with a nose.

There was an Old Man with a beard,
Who said, 'It is just as I feared! –
  Two Owls and a Hen,
  Four Larks and a Wren,
Have all built their nests in my beard!'

The Encyclopaedia Britannica remarks: 'Limericks have been composed upon every conceivable topic not excluding philosophy and religion.' And gives this example:

There was a young man who said 'Damn!
It is borne upon me that I am
  An engine which moves
  In predestined grooves,
I'm not even a bus; I'm a tram.'

The third and last great age and flourishing of the limerick (although it survives and is quite popular even today) was at the beginning of the century when there was a craze for limerick competitions, with newspapers offering huge prizes for clever ones and particularly for brilliant last lines (perhaps a reaction to Lear's dull and repetitive last lines).

The crop produced very few memorable pieces. E. V. K. remarks in the Britannica article: 'The judges in these competitions must have had poor ears, for scarcely any of the winning lines contained the correct number of feet.'

The clerihew is a modest cousin of the limerick but *its* origin is known perfectly well. It was invented and cultivated by E. Clerihew Bentley who was not only a well-known novelist but also the father of Nicolas Bentley, my recently dead and much lamented friend and the illustrator of many of my books. He also illustrated some of his father's clerihews – but not the ones published here.

> The people of Spain think Cervantes
> Equal to half-a-dozen Dantes:
> An opinion resented most bitterly
> By the people of Italy.

> Sir Humphry Davy
> Detested gravy.
> He lived in the odium
> Of having discovered Sodium.

> Karl Marx
> Was completely wrapped up in his sharks.
> The poor creatures seriously missed him
> While he was attacking the capitalist system.

And the most famous of all:

> The Art of Biography
> Is different from Geography.
> Geography is about Maps,
> But Biography is about Chaps.

# The Wittiest Englishman?

'A SECOND MARRIAGE is the triumph of hope over experience', said a young girl I knew, soon after my arrival in England. I was struck by the wit and the perfect, concise wording of the remark and said so.

'Oh, that's not by me,' she replied with a modest smile, 'it's by Dr Johnson.'

Now who was Dr Johnson? I had no idea. I was certainly no scholar of English literature but neither was I quite ignorant. I felt, from the way she mentioned him, that I ought to have known who Dr Johnson was. But I did not. My case was typical. Dr Johnson's name is often unknown to well-read Continentals who know all about the Brontës, Jane Austen, James Joyce, let alone Shakespeare and Shaw. The probable explanation is the fact that Dr Johnson was a greater talker than writer. His *Dictionary of the English Language* was a great achievement of lasting value; the *Lives of the Poets* and his *Journey to the Western Islands* are excellent, even if often pompous and ponderous, works; but he lives through his conversations. His luck – if to become immortal *is* luck and to be forgotten is not to be preferred – was to meet James Boswell, a man with an insatiable intellectual and, so to say, social appetite and gifted with a fabulous, tape-recording memory for conversations, which he put down in several volumes. He recorded the conversations of others, too; and other people sometimes recorded Johnson. The company he kept included many of the age's cleverest and most interesting men, and to listen to them was a great privilege. Dr Johnson had firm views on every subject under the sun, whether he knew something about it or not. But it did not really matter; even when he was talking rot it was brilliant rot. His views were always original; he expressed them with a few well-chosen words; his vocabulary – as befits a lexicographer – was rich and varied. His style of shooting was so impressive that it hardly mattered whether he hit the target or missed it.

Even if his name is not too well known on the Continent, at least one of his remarks is universally quoted: 'Patriotism is the last refuge of the scoundrel'. In a rather similar vein are the following reflections on the realities of warfare:

> The life of a modern soldier is ill represented by heroick fiction. War has means of destruction more formidable than the cannon and the sword. Of the thousands and ten thousands, that perished in our late contests with France and Spain, a very small part ever felt the stroke of an enemy; the rest languished in tents and ships, amidst damps and putrefaction; pale, torpid, spiritless, and helpless; gasping and groaning, unpitied among men, made obdurate by long continuance of hopeless misery, and whelmed in pits, or heaved into the ocean, without notice and without remembrance. By incommodious encampments and unwholesome stations, where courage is useless, and enterprise unpracticable, fleets are silently dispeopled, and armies sluggishly melted away.

He enjoyed making fun of the Scots whom he disliked and even despised. A Scotsman once remonstrated with him and observed that 'Scotland had a great many noble prospects.'

Johnson replied: 'Sir, you have a great many. Norway, too, has noble wild prospects; and Lapland is remarkable for prodigious noble wild prospects. But, Sir, let me

'The noblest prospect which a Scotchman ever sees is the high road
that leads him to England.'

tell you, the noblest prospect which a Scotchman ever sees is the high road that leads him to England.'

The flavour of his conversation may be best enjoyed if one reads a bit of continuous dialogue, with arguments and repartees.

He talked disparagingly of the work of Churchill, a celebrated poet of his times:

> JOHNSON: It has a temporary currency only from its audacity of abuse, and being filled with living names, and it will sink into oblivion.
>
> BOSWELL: You are hardly a fair judge, Sir; for Churchill has attacked you violently.
>
> JOHNSON: Nay, Sir, I am a very fair judge. He did not attack me violently till he found I did not like his poetry; and his attack on me shall not prevent me from continuing to say what I think of him, from an apprehension that it may be ascribed to resentment. No, Sir; I called the fellow a blockhead at first, and I will call him a blockhead still. However, I will acknowledge that I have a better opinion of him now than I once had; for he has shown more fertility than I expected. To be sure, he is a tree that cannot produce good fruit; he only bears crabs. But, Sir, a tree that produces a great many crabs is better than a tree which produces only a few.

Or take this not too convincing but very original defence of Christian truth. He, a firm believer, was talking of people who denied the truth of Christianity.

> It is always easy to be on the negative side. If a man were now to deny that there is salt upon the table, you could not reduce him to an absurdity. Come, let us try this a little farther. I deny that Canada is taken, and I can support my denial by pretty good arguments. The French are a much more numerous people than we; and it is not likely that they would allow

us to take it. 'But the ministry have assured us, in all the formality of the *Gazette*, that it is taken.' – Very true. But the ministry have put us to an enormous expense by war in America, and it is in their interest to persuade us that we have got something for our money. 'But the fact is confirmed by thousands of men who were at the taking of it.' – Ay, but these men have still more interest in deceiving us. They don't want that you should think the French have beat them, but that they have beat the French. Now, suppose you should go over and find that it really is taken, that would only satisfy yourself: for when you come home we will not believe you. We will say, you have been bribed. – Yet, Sir, notwithstanding all these plausible objections, we have no doubt that Canada is really ours. Such is the weight of common testimony. How much stronger are the evidences of the Christian religion?

But he did not approve all the aspects of devotion and piety. The talk was on religious orders.

It is as unreasonable for a man to go into a Carthusian convent for fear of being immoral, as for a man to cut off his hands for fear he should steal. There is, indeed, great resolution in the immediate act of dismembering himself: but when that is once done, he has no longer any merit; for though it is out of his power to steal, yet he may all his life be a thief in his heart. All severity that does not tend to increase good, or prevent evil, is absurd. I said to the Lady Abbess of a convent, 'Madam, you are here, not for the love of virtue, but the fear of vice.' She said, 'I shall remember this as long as I live.'

He could be very wise, even if somewhat unconventional, on love and marriage.

Talking of Mrs Careless, Johnson said: 'If I had married her, it might have been as happy for me.' – BOSWELL: 'Pray,

Sir, do you not suppose that there are fifty women in the world, with any one of whom a man may be as happy as with any one woman in particular?' – JOHNSON: 'Ay, Sir, fifty thousand.' – BOSWELL: 'Then, Sir, you are not of opinion with some who imagine that certain men and certain women are made for each other; and that they cannot be happy if they miss their counterparts.' – JOHNSON: 'To be sure not. Sir, I believe marriages would in general be as happy, and often more so, if they were all made by the Lord Chancellor, upon a due consideration of the characters and circumstances, without the parties having any choice in the matter.'

Today he would speak of a computer instead of the Lord Chancellor. And today he would be called a male chauvinist pig. Or perhaps not. Even the greatest men are products of their age and environment and today, probably, he would hold different views from his views of two hundred years ago. One day in 1763 Boswell told Johnson that he had been at a Quaker meeting and had heard a woman preach.

Johnson's comment was: 'Sir, a woman's preaching is like a dog's walking on his hinder legs. It is not done well; but you are surprised to find it done at all.'

Many people think Dr Johnson was the wittiest Englishman who ever lived. Others vote for Oscar Wilde – except, of course, that he was Irish, like that other great wit Bernard Shaw. Many of Wilde's aphorisms reflect an obvious desire to shine and were uttered *pour épater le bourgeois*. The formula is terribly out of date today. But fashions do change, and the paradox – never dead – will come back into vogue.

What's wrong with his assessment: 'The justification of a character in a novel is not that other persons are what they are, but that the author is what he is. Otherwise the novel is not a work of art.'

Or: 'Most of our modern portrait painters are doomed to absolute oblivion. They never paint what they see. They paint what the public sees, and the public never sees anything.'

On religious belief: 'The growth of common sense in the English Church is a thing very much to be regretted. It is really a degrading concession to a low form of realism. It is silly, too. It springs from an entire ignorance of psychology. Man can believe the impossible but man can never believe the improbable.'

And a last remark by Wilde: 'Formerly we used to canonize our heroes. The modern method is to vulgarize them. Cheap editions of great books may be delightful, but cheap editions of great men are absolutely detestable ... Every great man nowadays has his disciples but it is always Judas who writes the biography.'

I could add many other witticisms by many other writers: Shaw, Chesterton, Hilaire Belloc, Stephen Potter, Somerset Maugham – the list is very long and I like to keep my books rather short, so I shall resist temptation ... except for two little poems by Chesterton, a letter of Belloc's which throws an interesting light on his *Cautionary Tales*, and (pure self-indulgence, this) one of T. S. Eliot's delightful poems from *Old Possum's Book of Practical Cats*; all of which come at the end of this chapter.

To conclude these thoughts on the wittiest Englishman, I must declare a bias for my one and only hero who is more often thought of in his other roles: Winston Churchill. A. P. Herbert said of him as a humorist: 'If he had done nothing else, he could and would have made himself famous in this way alone,' and I agree. And I do not think that my hero-worship makes me lose my critical faculty vis-à-vis Churchill: he deserves our admiration.

Herbert also said that a mere procession of witticisms

in print may give a sense of inhumanity, like 'a lot of men marching past in "comic opera" uniforms', and this is true. No great man should be represented as a machine churning out witty remarks, and this would be particularly unjust to Churchill who was very human, cruel and compassionate, vindictive and generously forgiving, petty and magnanimous. After the war – he had just been ousted from the premiership – he met a Labour Member, Richard Stokes, in the smoking room of the House of Commons. Stokes had attacked him on many occasions during the war, asking penetrating, awkward and aggressive questions. Churchill put his hand on Stokes' shoulder: 'Of course I've forgiven you. Such hatred as I have – and it isn't much – I would rather reserve for the future than the past.' He moved on but turned back and spoke again the inimitable Churchillian words with the famous chuckle: 'A judicious and thrifty disposal of bile.'

He was not always so charitable. He could pretty well massacre a person with a remark. Of the meek-mannered and supposedly soft Attlee, who replaced him in 1945, he remarked: 'A sheep in sheep's clothing.'

His encounters with Lady Astor, in the thirties, are also famous. After some bitter exchanges in the House, Churchill – then a backbencher, in the wilderness – was standing in the lobby with a few cronies of his when Lady Astor was passing. Churchill stepped forward and told her: 'You are ugly.'

She was somewhat taken aback by this ungentlemanly remark and retorted: 'And you are drunk.'

Churchill nodded: 'True. But by tomorrow morning *I* shall be sober.'

After another acrimonious exchange, Lady Astor jumped to her feet in the Chamber and shouted: 'If the Rt Hon Gentleman were my husband I'd put poison in his tea.'

To which Churchill replied: 'If the Hon Lady were my wife, I would drink it.'

All this was – it had to be – spontaneous. Most of us can think of effective, occasionally even brilliant, repartees on the staircase as we leave some encounter, or an hour, a day, a week, a month later. When I was still a law student in Budapest someone offended and humiliated me deeply. His insult rankled and tormented me for years and years. Hardly a week passed without my recalling that scene with a great feeling of shame and a sense of defeat, and I thought this bitter, tormenting feeling would accompany me throughout my life. But twenty-two years later, in London, quite suddenly, I thought of a devastating reply. I laughed aloud with joy, although I was alone in the street. I repeated it several times, with great gusto. That will teach the bastard a lesson. The matter was settled; I was cured. The point is that to think of a devastating reply even twenty-two years later has its therapeutic and soothing effect; but to be able to jump to your feet in the House and give an instantaneous reply, in the hearing of the House, the country – indeed, thanks to Hansard, to proclaim it into eternity – must be the most satisfying feeling in the world.

Churchill's genius permitted him to make jokes on the most solemn and grandiose occasions. Addressing the Canadian Parliament at a dark hour of the war, he was referring to Hitler's threat of wringing Britain's neck like a chicken's. He paused. Everyone expected a defiant 'sweat-and-blood' reply, or a quotation from Byron or Housman. What he said, in a slightly changed tone, was: 'Some chicken; some neck.' This is not a witty joke. It is, in fact, a cheap music-hall joke. But uttered on that occasion, preceded and followed by solemn and world-shaking statements, it created a happy, liberating effect on a tense audience. It was masterly. The words in themselves are nothing; but *those* words, on *that* occasion spoken by *that* man, have become immortal.

A. P. Herbert describes another, equally solemn and, for Churchill, potentially even more dangerous occasion.* It happened during the no-confidence debate in 1942, after a series of shattering British defeats when a small but important 'Churchill must go!' movement became vociferous. The motion was: 'The House has no confidence in the central direction of the war.' Churchill was making his final speech on which his fate depended. Half-way through Hore-Belisha interrupted him: 'What about the Churchill tank?'

'This tank, the A.22,' Churchill replied a little later, 'was ordered off the drawing board, and large numbers went into production very quickly. As might be expected it had many defects and teething troubles, and when these became apparent, the tank was appropriately rechristened Churchill.'

There was a brief, polite laughter. He continued: 'The defects have now been largely overcome. I am sure that this tank will prove, in the end, a powerful, massive and serviceable weapon of war.'

A. P. Herbert, himself a Member of Parliament at the time, comments: 'At that, I remember, we laughed as if we had never laughed before. Some have said that the little joke, turned against himself, but yet obliquely an answer to the whole attack, took the sting and strength out of it.' Then he adds: '. . . the world seemed suddenly a better place, Rommel a menace no more, and Churchill the only man.'

Perhaps better jokes have been made by many a politician. But never by a Prime Minister, during a war, and fighting for his political life. And this joke could not have been made by the Prime Minister of any other

---

* *Churchill*, edited by Charles Eade, Hutchinson, 1953.

country – the whole scene is typically British. *What* is being said is important on all occasions; but not half as important as *when*, *how* and *by whom*. The wittiest remark in the world may in another age become a dud; a mediocre music-hall joke may (as we saw earlier) make history.

When Churchill paid his first war-time visit to President Roosevelt, he stayed in the White House. Roosevelt was always a little suspicious of Churchill, thinking him too clever by half and suspecting that Churchill wanted to use America to save the British Empire; which, of course, he did. On this occasion the two leaders were talking well into the night. Churchill returned to his own quarters, when Roosevelt had an afterthought – there was something else he wanted to add to the discussion – and wheeled himself into Churchill's suite. Churchill had already had a shower and came out stark naked to meet the President. Roosevelt was a shy and somewhat prudish man, obviously quite embarrassed. Churchill noticed this and reassured him: 'The Prime Minister of Great Britain has nothing to conceal from the President of the United States.'

And finally, just one more anecdote, showing Churchill's wit, wickedness and charm. Joe Kennedy, the later and late President John Kennedy's father, was US Ambassador to Britain during the war. At a ceremonial dinner Mrs Kennedy sat next to Churchill. She had innumerable children and grandchildren and believed in a curious theory: that she could never fail to interest anyone she met because at least one of her many offspring must fascinate him. On this occasion the Prime Minister had been talking to his other neighbour for a long time. It was towards the end of dinner that he turned to Mrs Kennedy, who said to him: 'I don't think, Mr Churchill, that I have told you anything about my grandchildren.'

To which Churchill replied: 'For which, Madam, I am infinitely grateful.'

## ELEGY IN A COUNTRY CHURCHYARD

*G. K. Chesterton*

The men that worked for England
They have their graves at home:
And bees and birds of England
About the cross can roam.

But they that fought for England,
Following a falling star,
Alas, alas for England
They have their graves afar.

And they that rule in England,
In stately conclave met,
Alas, alas for England
They have no graves as yet.

## THE ENGLISHMAN

*G. K. Chesterton*

St George he was for England,
And before he killed the dragon
He drank a pint of English ale
Out of an English flagon.
For though he fast right readily
In hair-shirt or in mail,
It isn't safe to give him cakes
Unless you give him ale.

St George he was for England,
And right gallantly set free
The lady left for dragon's meat
And tied up to a tree;
But since he stood for England
And knew what England means,
Unless you give him bacon
You mustn't give him beans.

St George he is for England,
And shall wear the shield he wore
When we go out in armour
With the battle-cross before.
But though he is jolly company
And very pleased to dine,
It isn't safe to give him nuts
Unless you give him wine.

# TO MAURICE BARING

*From Hilaire Belloc*

KING'S LAND
August 8th, 1921

I have begun to make a new sort of Rhymes for little Children. Zita Benson who is here and works for the Catholic Truth Society says I ought to publish the rhymes with them.
Here are some.

### The Wasp

Oh! Look! Mamma, a wasp is here!
It buzzes and it comes so near
I'm sure 'twill sting me by and by!
God-damn the Bloody Wasp say I!

*The Game of Cricket*

I wish you'd speak to Mary, Nurse,
She's really getting worse and worse.
Just now when Tommy gave her out
She cried and then began to pout

And then she tried to take the ball
Although she cannot bowl at all.
And now she's standing on the pitch,
The miserable little Bitch!

*Grandmamma's Birthday*

Dear Grandmamma, with what we give,
We humbly pray that you may live
For many, many happy years:
Although you bore us all to tears.

Like all Lyric Verse of the Epigrammatic type these will
need ceaseless revision before they are exact: but even rough
and early versions will give you an idea of the new method.

# HENRY KING

*Who chewed bits of String, and was early cut off in
Dreadful Agonies.*

*Hilaire Belloc*

The Chief Defect of Henry King
    Was chewing little bits of String.
At last he swallowed some which tied
    Itself in ugly Knots inside.
Physicians of the Utmost Fame
Were called at once; but when they came
They answered, as they took their Fees,

'There is no Cure for this Disease.
Henry will very soon be dead.'
His Parents stood about his Bed
Lamenting his Untimely Death,
When Henry, with his Latest Breath,
Cried—'Oh, my Friends, be warned by me,
That Breakfast, Dinner, Lunch, and Tea
Are all the Human Frame requires . . .'
With that, the Wretched Child expires.

# THE RUM TUM TUGGER

*T. S. Eliot*

The Rum Tum Tugger is a Curious Cat:
If you offer him pheasant he would rather have grouse.
If you put him in a house he would much prefer a flat,
If you put him in a flat then he'd rather have a house.
If you set him on a mouse then he only wants a rat,
If you set him on a rat then he'd rather chase a mouse.
Yes the Rum Tum Tugger is a Curious Cat –
  And there isn't any call for me to shout it:
    For he will do
    As he do do
      And there's no doing anything about it!

The Rum Tum Tugger is a terrible bore:
When you let him in, then he wants to be out;
He's always on the wrong side of every door,
And as soon as he's at home, then he'd like to get about.
He likes to lie in the bureau drawer,
But he makes such a fuss if he can't get out.
Yes the Rum Tum Tugger is a Curious Cat –
  And it isn't any use for you to doubt it:
    For he will do
    As he do do
      And there's no doing anything about it!

The Rum Tum Tugger is a curious beast:
His disobliging ways are a matter of habit.
If you offer him fish then he always wants a feast;
When there isn't any fish then he won't eat rabbit.
If you offer him cream then he sniffs and sneers,
For he only likes what he finds for himself;
So you'll catch him in it right up to the ears,
If you put it away on the larder shelf.
The Rum Tum Tugger is artful and knowing,
The Rum Tum Tugger doesn't care for a cuddle;
But he'll leap on your lap in the middle of your sewing,
For there's nothing he enjoys like a horrible muddle.
Yes the Rum Tum Tugger is a Curious Cat –
    And there isn't any need for me to spout it:
        For he will do
        As he do do
            And there's no doing anything about it!

# Farewell to English Humour

A SHORT WHILE AGO I published a book, called *How to be Decadent*,* which ended with these words: 'Thirty years ago I admired the English enormously but did not like them very much; today I admire them much less but love them much more.' I also said that in England the ruling class did not rule, the working class did not work and the middle class was not in the middle. 'If you are a worker you are not to work, if you are a solicitor you are not to solicit, if you are a street walker you are not to walk the streets, if you are the Lord Privy Seal you are not a Lord and if you are the Black Rod you most certainly are not black (nor, for that matter, are you a rod). This aspect of England seems to be unchanging and unchangeable. Quite recently the British have brought in a new holiday (the one and only Socialist act of a Socialist government): the First of May. This year (1979) the First of May was celebrated on the Sixth of May. Quaint. Queer. Endearing.'

But is it? Is it not time to be a little less queer and a shade less endearing? I said earlier in this book that the famous Jewish sense of humour got lost in transit to Israel. That is a good thing because the new state of Israel needs very different qualities from the self-effacing, self-mocking attitudes of East European Jewry. Circumstances in Britain have also changed, just as drastically

---

* André Deutsch, 1977.

as the circumstances of the Jews, and Britain, too, needs new qualities and a new spirit. Instead of being the Good Losers the British ought to become the Nasty Winners; instead of sophisticated self-mockery they ought to learn repulsive competitiveness; instead of the endearing understatement they must get into the habit of wild exaggeration; instead of the enchanting ability of laughing at themselves they ought to learn taking themselves seriously. And what about a few lessons in kicking the man who is down? When all these things are learnt, Britain will certainly be a less pleasant place to live in but it will have a chance to survive. Once we have risen again to the high living standards of East Germany, we may start regaining our tolerance, our self-mocking understatement and our inimitable ability of laughing at ourselves.

The English sense of humour is the most wonderful thing any nation can boast of; if Britain wants to survive as a leading industrial nation it must get rid of it without delay.

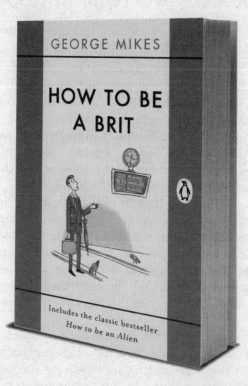

Read on for an extract of *How to be a Brit*,
the timeless and laugh-out-loud bestseller
from George Mikes on the quirks of
being British . . .

# I. How to be a General Alien

## A WARNING TO BEGINNERS

In ENGLAND* everything is the other way round.

On Sundays on the Continent even the poorest person puts on his best suit, tries to look respectable, and at the same time the life of the country becomes gay and cheerful; in England even the richest peer or motor-manufacturer dresses in some peculiar rags, does not shave, and the country becomes dull and dreary. On the Continent there is one topic which should be avoided – the weather; in England, if you do not repeat the phrase 'Lovely day, isn't it?' at least two hundred times a day, you are considered a bit dull. On the Continent Sunday papers appear on Monday; in England – a country of exotic oddities – they appear on Sunday. On the Continent people use a fork as though a fork were a shovel; in England they turn it upside down and push everything – including peas – on top of it.

On a continental bus approaching a request-stop the conductor rings the bell if he wants his bus to go on without stopping; in England you ring the bell if you want the bus to stop. On the Continent stray cats are judged individually on their merit – some are loved, some are only respected; in England they are universally worshipped as in ancient Egypt. On the Continent

* When people say England, they sometimes mean Great Britain, sometimes the United Kingdom, sometimes the British Isles – but never England.

*Sabbath morn*

people have good food; in England people have good table manners.

On the Continent public orators try to learn to speak fluently and smoothly; in England they take a special course in Oxonian stuttering. On the Continent learned persons love to quote Aristotle, Horace, Montaigne and show off their knowledge; in England only uneducated people show off their knowledge, nobody quotes Latin and Greek authors in the course of a conversation, unless he has never read them.

On the Continent almost every nation whether little or great has openly declared at one time or another that it is superior to all other nations; the English fight heroic wars to combat these dangerous ideas without ever mentioning which is *really* the most superior race in the world. Continental people are sensitive and touchy; the English take everything with an exquisite sense of humour – they are only offended if you tell them that they have no sense of humour. On the Continent the population consists of a small percentage of criminals, a small percentage of honest people and the rest are a vague transition between the two; in England you find a small percentage of criminals and the rest are honest people. On the other hand, people on the Continent either tell you the truth or lie; in England they hardly ever lie, but they would not dream of telling you the truth.

Many continentals think life is a game; the English think cricket is a game.

# INTRODUCTION

THIS is a chapter on how to introduce people to one another.

The aim of introduction is to conceal a person's identity. It is very important that you should not pronounce anybody's name in a way that the other party may be able to catch it. Generally speaking, your pronunciation is a sound guarantee for that. On the other hand, if you are introduced to someone there are two important rules to follow.

1. If he stretches out his hand in order to shake yours, you must not accept it. Smile vaguely, and as soon as he gives up the hope of shaking you by the hand, you stretch out your own hand and try to catch *his* in vain. This game is repeated until the greater part of the afternoon or evening has elapsed. It is extremely likely that this will be the most amusing part of the afternoon or evening, anyway.

2. Once the introduction has been made you have to enquire after the health of your new acquaintance.

Try the thing in your own language. Introduce the persons, let us say, in French and murmur their names. Should they shake hands and ask:

'Comment allez-vous?'

'Comment allez-vous?' – it will be a capital joke, remembered till their last days.

Do not forget, however, that your new friend who makes this touchingly kind enquiry after your state of health does not care in the least whether you are well and kicking or dying of delirium tremens. A dialogue like this:

HE:  How d'you do?

YOU:  General state of health fairly satisfactory. Slight insomnia and a rather bad corn on left foot. Blood pressure low, digestion slow but normal.

– well, such a dialogue would be unforgivable.

In the next phase you must not say 'Pleased to meet you.' This is one of the very few lies you must never utter because, for some unknown reason, it is considered vulgar. You must not say 'Pleased to meet you,' even if you are definitely disgusted with the man.

A few general remarks:

1. Do not click your heels, do not bow, leave off gymnastic and choreographic exercises altogether for the moment.

2. Do not call foreign lawyers, teachers, dentists, commercial travellers and estate agents 'Doctor'. Everybody knows that the little word 'doctor' only means that they are Central Europeans. This is painful enough in itself, you do not need to remind people of it all the time.

*Which hand will you have?*

# He just wanted a decent book to read ...

Not too much to ask, is it? It was in 1935 when Allen Lane, Managing Director of Bodley Head Publishers, stood on a platform at Exeter railway station looking for something good to read on his journey back to London. His choice was limited to popular magazines and poor-quality paperbacks – the same choice faced every day by the vast majority of readers, few of whom could afford hardbacks. Lane's disappointment and subsequent anger at the range of books generally available led him to found a company – and change the world.

*'We believed in the existence in this country of a vast reading public for intelligent books at a low price, and staked everything on it'*
**Sir Allen Lane, 1902–1970, founder of Penguin Books**

The quality paperback had arrived – and not just in bookshops. Lane was adamant that his Penguins should appear in chain stores and tobacconists, and should cost no more than a packet of cigarettes.

Reading habits (and cigarette prices) have changed since 1935, but Penguin still believes in publishing the best books for everybody to enjoy. We still believe that good design costs no more than bad design, and we still believe that quality books published passionately and responsibly make the world a better place.

So wherever you see the little bird – whether it's on a piece of prize-winning literary fiction or a celebrity autobiography, political tour de force or historical masterpiece, a serial-killer thriller, reference book, world classic or a piece of pure escapism – you can bet that it represents the very best that the genre has to offer.

## Whatever you like to read – trust Penguin.